TUSCANY
UMBRIA
L. Bolsena
Tuscania
Viterbo
Rieti
MAREMMA
CIMINI MTNS.
L. Vico
Tarquinia
SABATINI MTNS.
TOLFA MTNS.
L. Bracciano
Civitavecchia
Tiber R.
SABINE MTNS.
ABRUZZI
LAZIO
Roma
CIOCIARIA
ALBAN HILLS
Ostia
Sacco R.
Frosinone
(LATIUM)
Liri R.
Latina
MOLISE
CAMPANIA
TYRRHENIAN SEA
Mediterranean Sea
Gaeta
Gulf of Gaeta
Isole Ponziane
(Pontine Islands)
Roma
LAZIO
N

JULIA DELLA CROCE

ROMA

AUTHENTIC RECIPES FROM IN AND AROUND THE ETERNAL CITY

PHOTOGRAPHS BY PAOLO DESTEFANIS

CHRONICLE BOOKS
SAN FRANCISCO

For my loving godparents, Vince and Annette Messina

Library of Congress Cataloging-in-Publication Data:

Della Croce, Julia.
Authentic recipes from in and around the eternal city /
by Julia della Croce; photographs by Paolo Destefanis.
p. cm.
ISBN 0-8118-2352-0 (pbk.)
1. Cookery, Italian. 2. Cookery—Italy—Rome. I. Title.

TX723.D3972 2004
641.5945'632—dc21

Manufactured in Singapore.

Designed by Stuart McKee Design, San Francisco
Prop styling by Ester Chines
Food styling by Ester Chines and Paolo Destefanis
The photographer wishes to thank Paolo and Manola Terzuoli
of Altroieri Antiques, Pienza, Italy; Anna Bacchi Lega;
Fidia Cappelli's Linens, Monticchiello; Peggy Jaffe; and
Flavia Destefanis

Distributed in Canada by Raincoast Books
9050 Shaughnessy Street
Vancouver, British Columbia V6P 6E5

10 9 8 7 6 5 4 3 2 1

Chronicle Books LLC
85 Second Street
San Francisco, California 94105

www.chroniclebooks.com

CONTENTS

Introduction

ROME, VIA APPIA (THE APPIAN WAY), PORTA S. SEBASTIANO

The Romans built the via Appia in 312 B.C. In the words of the first-century A.D. poet Statius, it was "the queen of long roads." The famous highway was intended to bridge Rome and Naples and connect to the southern Adriatic ports, making way for a march on Magna Grecia. It has connected Rome to the south of Italy ever since.

Each of the five provinces grouped with Rome under the banner of Latium has its own particular history and, despite their ancient connections to the Empire, each has its own character. The reason for this goes back millennia. Rome imposed its rule on conquered territories for protection against outside attack, but it did not necessarily impose its culture. While the magistrates and other officials were, or became, Roman citizens, the common people in the ever-increasing colonies of the Empire carried on as before. Essentially, the hinterlands had a life of their own.

Who, then, are the people we now call Latians? The Etruscans are invariably credited with being the first to put down roots in central Italian soil, but as J. M. Roberts points out in his *History of the World*, "whenever they came to the peninsula and wherever from, Italy was then already a confusion of peoples." Indigenous groups were joined by tribes of Latins, Sabines, Umbri, Aequi, Volsci, and Indo-German (Italic) races, among others. The Latins built the first fortified settlements between the Tiber River and the Alban Hills. One of several small cities they founded was the nucleus of what would become Rome. Prior to and during Roman times, the Phoenicians zigzagged along the coastline selling their spices. The Etruscans carried on a lively trade with the Greeks, who sailed along Latium's coasts and set their footprints deep into Latium's soil.

It may be said that all ancient history flows into that of Rome, as into a river, flowing out into the sea; and that all modern history stems from the Romans. I will even go so far as to say that, had the Romans not existed, there would be no history to speak of.

—Leopold von Ranke,
nineteenth-century historian

The Ancient Roman Table

Historical accounts of the ancient Roman table conjure up a civilization whose gastronomical feats were as fantastic as its military ones. Exotic and precious ingredients were consumed in excess, made all the more remarkable by the form they took on the table. The grotesque culinary stunts of slave cooks, driven by the aristocracy, were designed to astonish and impress. Much has been written about gaudy Roman banquets with their offerings of live birds concealed in pies, a whole calf cleverly cooked so that it was boiled on one side and roasted on the other, dormice dripping with honey and rolled in poppy seeds, roasted peacocks served up in their plumage, and food cunningly disguised to look like something other than it was. Firsthand accounts tell of many multiple courses of elaborate if ridiculous delicacies served on dishes decorated with bronze, gold, and silver; wine poured into cups of hollowed semiprecious stones; and dinners offered on tables inlaid with ivory and draped with cloth of woven gold. Beautiful slaves and servants and bejeweled young boys served the food. There was nothing modest about such banquets, including the size of the guest lists. Caesar once invited sixty-nine thousand people for dinner, for which six thousand moray eels were procured for one of many dishes served.

I don't season a dinner the way other cooks do. They serve up a whole meadow in their dishes—they treat the guests like grazing cattle, shoving greens at them, then seasoning the greens with more greens. In go fresh coriander, fennel, garlic and alexanders, and on the side there's sorrel, cabbage, beet and blite: they pour a pound of silphium into it, and smash mustard seed in on top: stuff so fierce it makes their own eyes water before they've finished grinding it. When they cook a dinner they aren't flavoring it with seasonings, but with night-owls that are going to eat out your living intestines!

—A STAGE COOK, IN A COMEDY BY PLAUTUS (C. 250–184 B.C.), AS QUOTED IN *The Classical Cookbook*, BY ANDREW DALBY AND SALLY GRAINGER

Among the most valuable sources for studies of Roman culinary habits are the writings of Marcus Apicius, an erudite nobleman and gourmand who wrote the first recorded cookbook. Dishes that he created and cooked himself for his banquets made use of flamingo and parrot, lark's tongues, camel heels, ostrich, and sow's womb. After squandering the bulk of his inheritance, the equivalent of some four million dollars, on his culinary exploits and adventures, he committed suicide at the age of fifty-five, about A.D. 30, rather than risk simplifying his style of living (he slipped poison into his mouth only after finishing off a luxurious banquet).

Roman menus have lived into infamy for their shock value, but in fact, the dishes about which so much has been written were indulgences that only some two hundred households could afford. During the austere days of the Roman Republic, the puritan Cato the Elder *(Catone il Vecchio)*, who in 184 B.C. was elected the Republic's public censor, attempted to put an end to the decadence displayed by the city's nobility. In his writings, he urged a return to the cooking of the common people, which was by necessity largely cereal porridges *(pultes)*. For the ordinary Roman citizen, meat and fish, and even vegetables, were not easy to come by, and in any case, they were unaffordable.

Outside of the lavish, even scandalous, feasts indulged in by papal Rome, the eating habits of the Roman nobility died with the Empire. Neither Rome's cooking today, nor that of Latium, bears any resemblance to the gluttonous orgies of classical times. Today's Roman cooking evolved first from the traditions of the Greeks, and then from the culinary refinements of the Etruscans. It could be said that the Etruscans were the first to civilize Latium, even as Rome menaced, and ultimately gobbled, its kingdoms.

Questo [L'] amore per la tavola e
per la celebrazione di ogni avvenimento
intorno alla tavola bene imbandita
e sopratutto "coram populo," in nessuna
altra regione d'Italia era ed é ancora
oggi così evidente e così sentito.

More than any other region,
Lazio loves the table and celebrates
any important event around
the table. This is still very evident
and heartfelt and, above all,
it is universal among its people.

—Anna Gosetti della Salda,
Le ricette regionali italiane
(Regional Italian Recipes)

FACING PAGE:
Piazza del popolo in rome

The Roman genius was derivative rather than creative. It consisted of the ability to extract the best from the civilizations it conquered. From the Greeks and the Phoenicians, the Romans learned about farming. From the Etruscans, they learned to make wine, olive oil, and bread. During the period of the Roman Republic, the government provided free bread rations to its citizens. Along with *pultes*, bread became the staple of the poor. The cooking of Latium today is flavored with many of the aromatics borrowed from the Etruscan kitchen. Bay leaves, parsley, garlic, onion, basil, rosemary, mint, sage, celery, and marjoram are the predominant herbs; cloves and cinnamon are the favored spices. It was an Etruscan custom to eat not one main course, but many, one after the other, in order to extend the pleasures of the table. The Italian meal is still an extended feast, eaten leisurely, course by course.

The Contemporary Cooking of Latium

Most foreign travelers have wandered little into Latium's countryside, and have ventured even less into the realm of its cooking. Though the hinterlands have always been overshadowed by Rome, they retain their provincial differences, based on individual history and geography.

On the northern frontier is Viterbo Province. Many have sworn to have felt Etruscan ghosts hovering over the ruins of Viterbo city, Tarquinia, Vetralla, and other Etruscan sites. Certainly the cooking of this province is Etruscan at heart. It is natural and simple, connected to the bounty of the land, and keenly in tune with the change of seasons.

Viterbo shares the wild and wind-whipped sandy beaches of the Maremma with Tuscany, as well as that region's Etruscan heritage in most things, including the love of olive oil, on which its cooking is based (the rest of Latium has traditionally relied on

pork fat). The province takes in the Cimini Mountains, which straddle Latium and Umbria; Lake Bolsena, the largest volcanic lake in Italy; and a smaller lake, Vico. The lake districts have a cuisine of their own, based on freshwater fish cookery.

Rieti, once the land of the ancient Sabines, Latium's most northerly province, is squarely in Etruria. Sharing a border with Umbria, it is connected to it in both spirit and history. In Imperial times, the province was a Roman municipality. On the unification of Italy in 1860, it again became part of Umbria, but was annexed to Latium instead in 1927. Rieti Province falls within the Sabine Mountains, which accounts for its sturdy cooking and production of exceptional cured pork products, including mortadella, *guanciale,* and dried pork sausages. Like Umbria, its hillsides are carpeted with vineyards and olive groves.

The ancient coastal land of Latina, now the province of the same name, is steeped in legend and classical history. It was here, according to Virgil, that Ulysses and his crew were shipwrecked and met Circe, and here, on the glittering beaches, the Roman emperors built their summer homes (Tiberius had a stupendous villa where the sea laps the sand in Sperlonga, the foundation of which still stands; Lucullus had one near Monte Circeo). Latina is shaped by its ancient ties and its proximity to the sea, but also by the Pontine marshes, wetlands that were transformed by the Romans into fertile farmland. The marshes seeped back after the collapse of the Empire until some three hundred years ago, when immigrants from Padua, Venezia-Giulia, and Istria reclaimed the land. They created a system of canals, streets, and towns along Venetian lines, and like their northern countrymen, they favor seafood. In the Venetian spirit, the largest fish market in Italy has arisen in Terracina, on the nearby coast. The local waters are known for mullet, cod, sea bass, prawns, and *mazzancolle,* an exquisite variety of prawn that swims nowhere else in Italy besides

Latina's Bay of Gaeta and Veneto's Adriatic waters (where it is called *conòce* in the Venetian dialect). Also part of Latina is the *Isola di Ponza*, Pontine Island, famous for its tomatoes. The pastoral nature of the Latina-Campania border is reflected in a taste for lamb, game, smoked cheeses, and the famous *mozzarella di bufala* produced there.

Neighboring Frosinone, the only landlocked province of Latium, shares the pastoral and mountain cultures of bordering Abruzzo. Its olive oil and many types of handmade pastas are famous. The latter include *patacchi* ("farthings"), *sagne pelose* ("hairy" pasta made of whole wheat), and *ammazzacavalli* ("horse killers"). Matching sauces are based on artisanal sausages, meats, and hams. In the heart of Frosinone stretches the Ciociaria (a band of territory so named after the shape of the *ciocia*, the classic sandal of the ancient shepherds and bagpipers who roamed the mountains), a stupendous but unspoiled mountainous territory that takes in part of the Apennines, the Latium Subapennines, and the Sacco and Liri Rivers. According to mythology, its ancient towns and villages were founded by Saturn. It is here, muses the Italian writer Guido Piovene, that one finds the Latian landscape "in its pure state . . . spacious, silent, with large empty spaces. . . ." Frosinone, to which the Ciociaria territory more or less corresponds, has its own style of cooking based on its aromatic olive oil, white and black truffles, many wild mushroom varieties, chestnuts, unique cheeses, prosciutti, and *salumi* (cured meats), and its own breads and desserts.

FACING PAGE:
ANCHOVY FILETS IN A PAN WITH OLIVE OIL AND GARLIC

Rome, the province, takes in a broad stretch of countryside that today is intensely cultivated. The Campagna Romana, which runs along the Tiber, produces superb vegetables and fruits from its volcanic soil. Among the fertile Alban Hills are scattered the medieval Castelli Romani towns of wine fame. Tivoli is renowned both for its waterfalls and its pasta. Anzio was the birthplace of both Caligula and Nero, but also of savory pasta pie. The mountain towns spread tables with wild mushrooms and game, trout from nearby rivers, *abbacchio* (baby lamb), sheep cheeses, sausages, and a traditional array of cured pork products. There is both seafood and freshwater fish cooking. Ostia Antica, the original major port of Rome, is known for its fish trattorias and seafood specialties. The trattorias of Civitavecchia, the biggest seaport in Lazio today, are also famous for their seafood. Inland, the waters of Lake Bracciano are full of trout and pike among other freshwater fishes, which are served up in typical simplicity by the eating places scattered around the lake.

Più se spenne e pejo se magna.

The more you spend,
the worse you eat.

—Roman proverb

Then there is Rome itself, which the Italians always say has no cuisine of its own. This is not entirely true. There are commonalities between the cooking of Rome the city and Rome the province, but there are also distinctions. One is Rome's aggressive use of pepper. Another is its propensity for other bold flavors in spicing foods. A third is a cuisine based on lard and other pork fat, although this has given way in recent times to the lively flavored extra-virgin olive oil the region produces. What is lacking in refinement is compensated for by imagination. There is a particular taste for fennel, mint, cinnamon, and cloves, echoes of the ancient Roman love of spices. Other flavors largely unique to Rome are cilantro, bitter chocolate as a flavoring in meat stews, and sweet-and-sour dishes (Sicily and Venice are exceptions in the sweet-and-sour category).

Rome has preserved its traditional cooking both in the home kitchen and in the informal trattorias, despite the international influences on the city. Perhaps the many fashions and trends to which the city has been exposed over the centuries have reinforced the locals' attachment to things Roman, particularly in matters of the kitchen. The Italian culinary writer Felice Cúnsolo puts it this way: "Creating their own cuisine, the Romans have diligently

Le donne, fiere e combative quanto i loro uomini, mal si adattavano a stare davanti ai fornelli.

The [Roman] women, fiery and combative like their men, were maladapted to standing in front of the stoves.

—Anna Gosetti della Salda, *Le ricette regionali italiane (Regional Italian Recipes)*

safeguarded themselves from infiltrations and adulterations, just like those conquerors who guard their booty ferociously from the assaults of others."

It could be said that the spirit of the ancient Romans still prevails in the raucous outdoor markets, and also in their style of dining. The Romans love lavish displays of food and conviviality at the table. In a word, Roman cooking is lusty, and it is eaten with remarkable gusto. Years ago, I took a friend to Rome for her first visit. It was quite late at night when we finally made our way to a backstreet trattoria where "real" Romans gather to eat real Roman food. My friend sat for some time, menu in hand, but eyes fixed on the eating scene around us. When I asked her what could be distracting her from immediately putting in an order for dinner, she remarked, "Look at the way people are eating—as if they would jump right into their plates!" True enough, everyone around us seemed to be gesticulating wildly, arguing passionately, and filling the air with their voices all at once. They ate with their heads close to the table, forks poised to deliver food from plate to mouth by the shortest route, all with great zest and conviviality. As Bruno Rossi, the Italian food writer, says, "One way to know Romans best is to meet them at dinner."

EST! EST!! EST!!!
DI MONTEFIASCONE
€ 4,65
SECCO
VINCI VINI
ZIBIBBO

i vini laziali

The Wines of Latium

Chi manga senza beve, mura a secco.
Eating without drinking is like building without mortar.

— Roman saying

Montefiascone, "Fazi Trape' Luigi" wine shop

We know from fossil finds that grapes grew wild in Italy fifty-two million years ago. Further digging places their first transformation into wine in Etruria, what is now Latium, Umbria, and Tuscany, from the seventh to the fifth centuries B.C. Whether through their genius, or because of know-how imported from wherever they came, the Etruscans laid the foundations of Italian viticulture. The enthusiastic studies by the Romans of both Etruscan and Greek methods found expression in vines that carpeted the valleys and clung to the hillsides, from the Roman fields to Gaul, Spain, Britain, and beyond. Enough wine was produced in Latium to fill the glasses of all the Roman citizenry, including handouts to the poor, with enough left over to export. The authors of *Handbook to Life in Ancient Rome* write that "huge quantities of [wine] amphorae have been found stacked in the holds of wrecked [Roman] ships. . . . It is estimated that [they] carried [wine cargo] weighing 225 . . . to 600 long tons."

After Roman civilization and its wine presses were destroyed by successive waves of barbarians, Latium's monasteries resumed the cult of the vine. The good monks, wanting to fill the papal goblet as well as their own, enlisted no fewer than seven patron saints to bless their efforts. In order, they were St. Barnabas for the grapevines, St. Urbino for the grape harvest, St. Vincent for the wine growers, St. John for the grape must, St. Luke for the *vino nuovo* (new wine), St. Theodore for the taverns, and last but not least, St. Martin for the wine drinkers. St. Albert, né Alberto da Butrio, who was canonized for transforming water into wine in the presence of the pope and three cardinals, was thrown in for good luck. With the help of the heavens, there was so much wine that everyone's cup was once again full to the brim. By the Renaissance, the country roads were thick with *carrettieri* hauling barrels of wine to Rome. Latium's brisk wine trade resumed where it had left off. An anonymous Italian wine expert writing in *Guida rapida al gusto*, a guide to Italian food and drink, explains, "The great problem with Latium's wines is, and always has been, Rome—a city that, two thousand years ago, was already a metropolis capable of absorbing all the wine that landed in the the city's taverns, regardless of its quality and its source."

Wine comforts hope.

—Aristotle

Only after the modernization of Italy in the twentieth century were new techniques for viticulture developed. The establishment of DOC *(denominazione di origine controllata)* regulations forced producers to conform to rigorous standards in wine making, bringing about a virtual revolution in Italy's wines, including those of Latium. The DOC laws retired the services of some of the patron saints. They govern the production of wine from vineyard to aging cellar, protecting the name and reputation of wines.

The flask weeps when it is empty.

—Italian saying

Today's wines from Latium are more refined, if still robust and carefree, reflecting the region's intrinsic southern temperament. But the typical wine-loving foreigner, dazzled by French, Tuscan, and northern Italian labels, is often reticent to try them. A case in point is my own sister, an expatriate American who has lived in France for over three decades. When she visits our relations in Cervèteri (home of three DOC reds), she always brings her own (French) wine to drink—she has yet to try anything local.

All of Latium's provinces make wines, reds and whites alike, although the region's strength is in the latter. Montefiascone's Est! Est! Est! and Frascati have international reputations, but the whites of the Castelli Romani ("Roman castles," after the thirteen castles that crown the medieval towns on the Alban Hills east of Rome), especially Marino, which has had somewhat of a cult following among the Romans and is widely exported, are distinguished. Less well known abroad, but neck and neck in local popularity, are other labels from the Alban Hills, including Colli Albani, Castelli Romani, Velletri whites, Colli Lanuvini, and Montecompatri Colonna. Everyone who knows white Orvieto, the ancient and celebrated wine of bordering Umbria, will be familiar with the Orvieto whites produced on Latium's side of the border, around Bolsena. In addition to reds, the aforementioned Cervèteri in Rome Province turns out an agreeable white wine designed for drinking with the local seafood and lake fish.

South of Rome, in the remote medieval landscape close to the mountainous Frosinone Province, three substantial reds with good reputations are bottled under the Cesanese label. Other dry reds are made in Aprilia, in Latina Province.

In sum, there are fine wines as well as simple wines of the region, which have their charms. Latium's wines were designed for casual drinking, and their flavors are best appreciated with the humble and vigorous dishes of the region.

la dispensa laziale

The Pantry of Latium

Fresh peas and pods

Visitors seek out the monuments and sites of ancient Rome and are amazed. They linger there awhile, taking in the architecture, the air, the people, and the opulence of the Eternal City, and remember them forever. But they cannot take any of it away with them. Certainly, they cannot taste them. Anyone seriously interested in the culture of Rome can, though, savor the marvels of its table by sampling the cheeses, cured meats, and other local specialties sold in the food stalls of the outdoor markets and in the many lovely shops where fresh produce and artisanal foods are sold.

There are foods particular to Rome and Latium of which readers should have a working knowledge, whether their interest is in reproducing authentic regional dishes at home, or whether they intend to enjoy Roman and Latian food properly on site. Just as we like to have a guide to direct us to the most interesting attractions and the best restaurants, we like to know what we are eating when we are on foreign soil. Some products listed here are universally Italian, but they are included because they have roots in Rome or in Latium, or a particular connection to the region's cooking. If you visit there, go into a market or shop and buy some of the *salumi,* cheeses, olives, and other provisions of the region, and eat them at once. You will marvel at how much better they taste on their home soil and at their freshest, than when they are exported abroad.

The Latian kitchen is based on a modest pantry, simple dishes, and a cooking style rooted in the traditions of commoners and simple country people.

Cheeses *(formaggi e latticini)*

Because Latium has been a pastoral culture since ancient times, cheese has always been central to the diet of Rome and its outlying territories. During the Empire, the breakfast of the typical Roman man consisted of bread, cheese, and wine, while that of the woman was of bread, cheese, and milk. Latium is still cheese country.

The first distinction to make is between aged cheeses, *formaggi,* and fresh cheeses, *latticini.* Aged cheeses are molded in a form, while fresh cheeses are made *a pasta filata:* pulled by hand to separate the solids from the whey.

There are two primary aged cheeses of the region, *pecorino romano* and *provola,* and two fresh cheeses: *ricotta romana* and *mozzarella di bufala.* There are also numerous artisanal aged and fresh cheeses from locality to locality. Sadly, they have decreased in recent decades as Latium has modernized and the cheese maker's craft has drawn fewer and fewer young people. DOP legislation has also made some of the artisanal cheeses obsolete as the demand for *pecorino romano* DOP has increased. Nevertheless, when traveling outside of Rome, it is worthwhile to pop into *salumerie* and small *latticini* (fresh-cheese shops) where local cheeses are sold. You will inevitably come across charming local *formaggi* and *latticini* whose production may be a dying art. I have mentioned one or two in this section, but many more could be included.

FACING PAGE:
ROME, CAMPO DEI FIORI, PARKED HAND-PUSHED CARTS

Pecorino romano **(DOP):** *Pecora* means "sheep" in Italian, thus pecorino is sheep's cheese. It is primordial shepherd's food, and one of Latium's oldest cheeses. Because it keeps well, it was a staple of the Roman legions. The same type of cheese is produced in Sardinia *(pecorino sardo)* and Tuscany *(pecorino toscano,* or *caciotta),* but it originated in Latium. The method for making *pecorino romano* from fresh sheep's milk, salt, and lamb rennet mentioned in the first-century A.D. work *De re rustica* is essentially the same method that is used today. *Pecorino romano* is Latium's most important product for export.

Pecorino romano is lightly salty and rustic in character. Its sharpness is related to its period of maturation, which ranges from five months for a table cheese to a range of nine months to a year for grating purposes. Outside of Italy, it is typically used interchangeably with the more refined and complex parmigiano-reggiano. To reproduce the genuine flavor, *pecorino romano* should be used rather than parmigiano-reggiano cheese. What is exported to America is the aged varieties, which are suitable primarily for grating over certain pasta dishes. Young, mild pecorino has many uses in cooking, particularly in certain baked dishes where a melting cheese is necessary but where mozzarella would be too bland. Do not attempt to substitute aged pecorino for its young relatives in recipes that call for the latter; it is too sharp for these purposes. Although not as refined as parmigiano-reggiano, young, mild pecorino also makes a good table cheese.

Mozzarella di bufala campana **(DOP)** is produced in the "buffalo lands" of thirteen provinces of Frosinone, nineteen provinces in Latina, and six provinces of Rome (its important production in neighboring Campania accounts for its name). The water buffalo has been a part of the landscape in parts of Latium since the twelfth century, but full-scale production of this cheese did not begin until the eighteenth century. Today, both regions produce it.

20

I once mentioned to a young Italian friend of mine, in the heart of the mozzarella country . . . that it was my habit to buy mozzarella from my local grocer at about 4 P.M., when the cheese arrived from a nearby dairy, and to eat it the next day. "Ah, you see," he replied with a pained expression, "it is very difficult for me, who grew up here, to eat a mozzarella that is more than two-and-a-half-hours old."

—William Murray,
"St. Francis of the Buffalo,"
Saveur

FACING PAGE:
Water buffalo, whose milk is used in mozzarella-making, in the Fondi, Latina province

A tender, round, unripened fresh cheese, *mozzarella di bufala* has a very thin, glossy skin. You will find it formed into balls, braids, or small *bocconcini,* "mouthfuls." If you buy it from a mozzarella maker who really knows his craft, he will tell you that it should be eaten within hours after it is made in order to experience its true flavor: slightly tangy, unlike the comparatively bland fresh mozzarella made from cow's milk. At the least, it should be eaten on the same day. Because it is ruined when exposed to refrigeration, genuine *mozzarella di bufala campana* cannot really be exported. Unless labeled *"di solo latte di bufala,"* virtually all fresh mozzarellas sold outside of Latium and Campania are made of cow's milk or a mix of buffalo and cow milk. Both versions are eaten uncooked, or used in cooking.

Provola, or *provatura,* originates in the south of Italy, but this rustic cheese has caught on in Latium. Not to be confused with provolone, its aged relative, it is a smaller, egg-shaped cheese made *a pasta filata,* by the "pulled-curd" method also used in making mozzarella. Because it is aged no more than eight days, it is mild and semisoft. The best *provola* is made from water buffalo's milk, but today it is also produced from cow's milk. *Provola* also comes in smoked varieties, and is both an eating cheese and a cooking cheese. The variations can be found in well-stocked Italian food shops in the United States, or ordered from purveyors listed in Mail-Order Sources (page 157).

Scamorza is also made by the "pulled-curd" method. A pear-shaped, soft but firm cheese made of whole cow's milk, or sometimes of combined cow's milk and sheep's milk, *scamorza* has a creamy, delicate flavor made all the more appealing when it is flavored with bits of black truffle during the truffle harvest. In Rome it is grilled until seared on the outside and runny inside, and eaten for a *secondo* (second course) in place of meat or fish. *Scamorza* is sold in well-stocked Italian food shops in the United States, or it can be ordered (see Mail-Order Sources, page 157).

Ricotta romana: The classic *ricotta romana* made from sheep's milk is considered the best in Italy. Along with *pecorino romano,* it is the oldest cheese of Latium, distinguished from other ricottas by its thickness and superior flavor. *Ricotta romana* is eaten fresh, for breakfast on *pizza bianca* (white pizza), or used as a main ingredient in puddings, cakes, and pies. It is even made into gelato, Italy's famed ice cream. The other form it takes is dried, salted ricotta, called *ricotta salata,* which is used as an eating cheese or grated over certain pasta dishes. Where true *ricotta romana* is not available, cow's milk ricotta can be substituted, but it should be drained in a cheesecloth-lined sieve in the refrigerator for several hours or overnight to remove excess water.

Chestnuts *(castagne)*

The early Romans planted chestnut trees everywhere they would grow, and grow they did. One of them, planted in Sicily, flourished for over two thousand years until Mount Etna covered it with lava in 1850. The Cimini Mountains in Viterbo Province have long blossomed with chestnut trees. Every October there are festivals to celebrate the chestnut harvest, and vendors with baskets full of them appear on the streets and by roadsides, selling them uncooked or roasted. Once, I bought a basket of freshly picked chestnuts from an old woman at the entrance of a beautiful old church on a hilltop in Tuscia. Happily, the cottage I had rented came with a fireplace—and a traditional chestnut-roasting basket—so I was able to cook them over an open fire. The freshly harvested chestnuts were a revelation: sweet, moist, and meaty, unlike the chestnuts we get at home, which have traveled far before they appear in our markets. At harvesttime, the fresh nuts can turn up in anything from soup to goose stuffing, marmalade, and confections. The bulk of them are dried like beans for future rehydration, ground into chestnut flour for baking, or bottled in purée or whole form for export to pricey specialty food shops abroad. The imported frozen chestnuts that have become available in recent years are, to my mind, the best alternative to fresh ones, but they can be hard to find.

Chickpeas *(ceci)*

Chickpeas, or *ceci* (called *garbanzos* in Spanish), bear mention. For one thing, they have grown in parts of Italy at least since the time of Neolithic man. They were a saving grace for the Romans, there being little else to eat at bleak points of their history. When Horace wrote "*inde domum me ad porri et ciceris refero, laganique catium,*" or roughly, "I am going home to a bowl of leeks, chickpeas, and lasagne (broad noodles)," it might have been his only course. Besides Horace's recipe, a typical treatment was to cook them with garlic or onion and pork fat. The food journalist Waverly Root writes that chickpeas and pork fat were "the pork and beans of the ancient world, canned (in amphorae) in Pompeii and exported to the rest of Roman territory." Romans have never tired of chickpeas. *Pasta e ceci*, pasta and chickpeas, is still one of their favorite dishes.

Cooking Chickpeas: Canned chickpeas acquire an unpleasant flavor in the can. It is best to rehydrate them in their dried form. Here is the method: Purchase dried chickpeas from an ethnic market where there is a brisk turnover in business. (When dried beans or chickpeas sit on the shelf for more than nine months or so, they become tough, even when rehydrated.) Rinse them well and put them in a pan. For 1 cup of chickpeas, add 5 cups of cold water and 1/8 teaspoon baking soda. Cover and leave in a cool place for 12 to 15 hours. Drain and rinse. Put them in a pan with 6 cups of water. Bring to a boil, then reduce the heat to a simmer and cook until tender, about 1 to 1 1/2 hours. If necessary, cook them longer. Add 1 teaspoon salt. Let stand for 15 minutes for the salt to be absorbed.

Emmer *(farro)*

Farro originated in Neolithic times. The grains of this ancient form of wheat resemble those of wheat berries, but they are a deeper brown color, and slightly more oblong and tapered. In early Roman times, *farro* was ground into flour with a stone grinding device and cooked into a porridge in an *olla,* what we would call a kettle. It was still cooked in the primordial way, except that when meat became less scarce, it was cooked in broth. When, in the second century B.C., the Roman Republic's elected censor Cato the Elder decried the gastronomical excess of the city's nobility, there was a revival of interest in *farro. Farro* was eventually replaced with modern wheat, but there has been a revival of its use in modern times.

Farro can be purchased in its whole-berry form or ground into a meal the consistency of very coarse cornmeal. The whole berries are prepared just as dried beans are: soaked, then boiled until they are fairly tender but not mushy. In their whole form, they are added to soups or, since the *farro* revival, made into salads (akin to the Middle Eastern cracked-wheat salad called *tabbouleh*), just as beans are. They can be cooked directly in a soup broth as for Farro and Cabbage Soup *(zuppa di cavolo e farro),* page 60.

In its ground form, *farro* doesn't need soaking. It is cooked in salted water just like polenta, or for more flavor, in broth, to serve as a bed for meat or stews. The most pleasant way to cook it, to my taste, is in vegetable or chicken soup in place of soup pasta.

Lard *(strutto)*

Lard has been the region's primary cooking fat since Roman times, when the pig was highly regarded. It is still the flavor foundation of many Roman dishes, although olive oil is fast replacing it.

Lentils *(lenticchie)*

Onano, Grotte di Castro, and San Lorenzo Nuovo (Viterbo) grow lentils characterized by their tender skins. Typical lentil dishes are Rome's famous lentil and sausage soup, lentil and pasta soups, and lentils cooked in a *battuto* of chopped garlic or onion, carrot, celery, and parsley, with sausages. Lentils (symbolizing coins) and *cotechino* sausage is a dish traditionally served throughout the region on New Year's Day to bring abundance.

MEATS

Cured Meats *(salumi)*

Cured meats are called *salumi* in Italian, which comes from the Latin word *salumen*, "salted food." *Salumi* are as old as Latium itself, going back to times when people needed to salt foods in order to preserve them for future use. Their use was widespread in ancient Greece and Rome, where the artisans who produced them, the *cupedinari*, were respected craftsmen. The word *prosciutto* originates from the Vulgar Latin *peresxuctus*, meaning "without liquid." A first-century Roman cookbook entitled *De re rustica*, by Marcus Portius Cato, records the first recipe for making prosciutto. It is the same recipe that is used today throughout central and southern Italy.

The tradition of making dried sausages *(salami)* also goes back to Roman times when the upper Tiber Valley, now northern Lazio and Umbria, was already renowned for making them. In ancient Rome, both prosciutto and salami were made of boar meat and pork meat.

Coppiette: From *coppia*, meaning "couple," these are fiery dried *salami* made of horsemeat and tied into a pair, thus the name.

Guanciale: This form of salt pork from the jowl is a favorite cooking fat in many parts of Latium and is considered indispensable in *spaghetti all'amatriciana*. It comes rolled up, like pancetta, which by necessity must substitute for it in the United States (*guanciale* is not exported), but has a distinctly stronger flavor.

Mortadella di Amatrice, like the mortadellas of other regions, is made of finely ground and spiced pork speckled with bits of white fat and formed into long sausages. Amatrice specializes in making it.

Prosciutto laziale: Bassiano and Guarcino specialize in the production of prosciutto.

Salsiccia di Monte San Biago: A pleasant pork sausage flavored with coriander and red pepper that is a specialty of Monte San Biago, Fondi, and Itri in the province of Latina.

Fresh Meat Specialties

Abbacchio: It is a toss-up as to whether Latians like *porchetta* or *abbacchio* more, but more often than not, *abbacchio* would win. This is milk-fed baby lamb, so tender that it goes down the throat like butter. In the past, *abbacchio* was reserved for the Easter feast for its Christian symbolism of new life, but today it is eaten year-round.

Porchetta, spit-roasted milk-fed baby pig is ubiquitous throughout Latium. The Umbrians lay claim to having been the first to cook it, and to flavor it with rosemary and wild fennel as the Romans do. In any case, *porchetta* was sold as street food in ancient times. Today, *porchetta* cooking on portable spits is a familiar sight in Rome and Latium, indeed throughout central Italy. After cooking, it is sliced warm and offered between two slices of bread.

Vitellone bianco dell'Appennino Centrale **(IGP)** is meat from the white cattle of the central Apennine region. This tender meat is exceptionally tasty while at the same time being low in fat. The animals graze on the grasses, wild herbs, and flora of meadows and fields, and are raised without growth hormones or antibiotics. *Vitellone,* meaning adult veal, refers to young male or female cattle between twelve and twenty-four months old. IGP, *Indicazioni Geografiche Protette,* is a government label for agricultural products that are organically raised in designated geographic areas with a common origin and history. Latium falls in the central Apennine region, in which three breeds of *vitellone* can be bred to meet regulated government standards: Val di Chiana, Marchigiana, and Romagnola.

FACING PAGE: TURTLE FOUNTAIN, PIAZZA MATTEI

Olives *(olive da tavola)*

Gaeta is famous for its black variety of table olives, which are exported in large number. Their pleasantly bitter flavor makes them suitable for cooking with the fruity Italian plum tomatoes used for sauces, or tossed into the stew pot with mild-flavored meats such as chicken or rabbit, where they add a burst of tartness. A famous olive specialty, called *olive ascolane* (because the recipe originated in Ascoli-Piceno in the bordering Marches region), calls for huge green San Gregorio olives stuffed with ground beef or pork, and fried.

Olive Oil *(olio extravergine laziale)*

Olive trees have been part of the Latian landscape since pre-Roman history dating to the Etruscan civilization and possibly earlier. In Imperial Rome, the houses of both rich and poor had olive presses. The oldest living olive-producing trees in Italy grow in the soft silvery hills of Viterbo Province, and in the ancient olive groves of Sabina (Rieti Province). The climate of both Canino and Sabina is mild, and the slopes of the hills provide good drainage, factors that figure in the oil's refined yet flavorful character.

The mystique of Tuscan and Ligurian *olio d'oliva* has dominated markets outside Italy's borders for many years, but *olio extravergine d'oliva Canino* (DOP), and *olio extravergine d'oliva Sabina* (DOP) are highly ranked. The DOP mark is bestowed only on extra-virgin olive oils derived from particular olives. Canino DOP is produced from different olive cultivars than Sabina DOP, which give it different flavor and aroma characteristics.

Extra-virgin olive oil Canino DOP is green-gold with a crisp and fruity aroma and a bold and peppery flavor. Extra-virgin olive oil Sabina (DOP) is golden yellow with a green cast. Its aroma is fruity and its flavor assertive but silky, highly scented, and sweet. The Sabina DOP designation dictates that the oil must be produced within the boundaries of Sabina, which takes in parts of Rieti Province and Rome Province.

Like other good extra-virgin olive oils, these oils are obtained by traditional methods of cold pressing from local olives harvested within the previous twenty-four hours. Oils pressed from olives that are stored any longer are exposed to fermentation and, by definition, cannot yield extra-virgin olive oil of less than 1 percent acidity.

Polenta *(polenta laziale)*

The basic method for cooking polenta is the same in Lazio as elsewhere in Italy, but there are provincial variations on how it is served. Not surprisingly, it makes its appearance in Lazio's mountain regions as a porridge alongside pungent wild greens cooked with plenty of garlic and hot red pepper, or with succulent, saucy stews of pork ribs (page 87). Lazio's rustic cheeses are pleasant, with a nutty flavor and grainy texture. A big lump of butter and slices of sweet or smoked *provola* might dress a steaming mound of polenta, but the simplest local treatment is sweet butter and a generous veil of grated sheep's cheese.

I borghiciani (abitanti del bel quartieredi Borgo), sono stati grandi mangiatori di polenta. Chi lo dice? Beh, le campane di S. Pietro e di S. Maria in Traspontina. Le seconda domandano a mezzogiorno "Indò se magna la polenta?" E il campanone di S. Pietro pontifica tonante "In Borgo, in Borgo, in Borgo!"

The residents of the Borgo district were great polenta eaters. Says who? Well, its church bells. At noon the bells of Saint Mary in Traspontina ask, "Where can we eat polenta?" and the big bells of Saint Peter's Basilica pontificate with a thunder, "In Borgo, in Borgo, in Borgo . . . "

—As quoted in *La cucina regionale italiana*, by Marina Colacchi and Pino Simone

If you cannot find genuine imported Italian cornmeal for polenta, Spanish cornmeal marketed by Goya and other Latin food companies can be substituted. There is an imported Italian instant polenta that cooks in five minutes, but it is expensive and it thickens and cooks so quickly that lumps form even as it is stirred. It is important not to confuse the type of ordinary cornmeal used for muffins and the like with polenta cornmeal, as it will only produce a nasty sludge.

There are both coarse and fine varieties of polenta, and yellow and white varieties. The coarse variety is more suitable for slicing and grilling after it is cooked. The yellow type is sometimes called *farina rossa di granturco,* literally "red" corn flour. Coarse meal produces a gritty, rustic polenta that the Italians say can be felt *sotto i denti,* "under the teeth," and it typically has more corn flavor than does fine-ground polenta. Either type can be served simply with butter and cheese, or topped with a meat sauce or stew.

Truffles *(tartufi)*

The ancient Romans considered white truffles a gift from the gods, attributing magical and love-inducing properties to them. Black truffles, on the other hand, were not eaten because they were thought to be a medium for black magic. Today, both varieties are prized, though Latium does not have nearly the prodigious truffle harvest of its northerly neighbor Umbria. Enough black truffles grow in the cooler and more sheltered part of the region to satisfy the local appetite for them. A lovely dish I ate in Bracciano comes to mind: delicate handmade ravioli stuffed with truffle-specked ricotta.

Vegetables and Herbs *(verdura e erbe)*

Artichokes *(carciofi):* All of Italy loves artichokes, particularly Venice and Sardinia, but Lazio elevates cooking them to an art form. Among the superior artichoke varieties that Lazio grows is the *cimarolo romano,* also called the *mammola* artichoke. It is a clear green tinted with violet, with a thick and fleshy straight stem. This delicious specimen probably reaches its height of gastronomical glory in *carciofi alla giudia* (artichokes in the Jewish style): Its outer leaves are stripped, its stem is removed, and a skilled hand using a small knife makes cuts from base end to tip rotating the thistle all the while, like a pot on a potter's wheel. After this treatment, the chokes are soaked in water and lemon juice for a bit, then turned upside down on a wooden surface where they can be whacked with a swift, bold chop in order to flatten and spread the leaves open somewhat. They are slipped into the skillet upside down and fried in hot olive oil while being constantly turned, until little by little the outer artichoke grows golden brown, the leaves turn crunchy, and the flesh becomes tender to the heart. At the end, the artichoke is turned in the pan, pressed open with a metal spatula, and shocked with a spray of cold water. At this point the artichokes nearly leap out of the pan and onto a plate, begging to be eaten, but not before a sprinkling of sea salt can be made. I have not offered the recipe in the vegetable chapter because by and large,

FACING PAGE:
ROME, CAMPO DE' FIORI, CLEANING ARTICHOKES

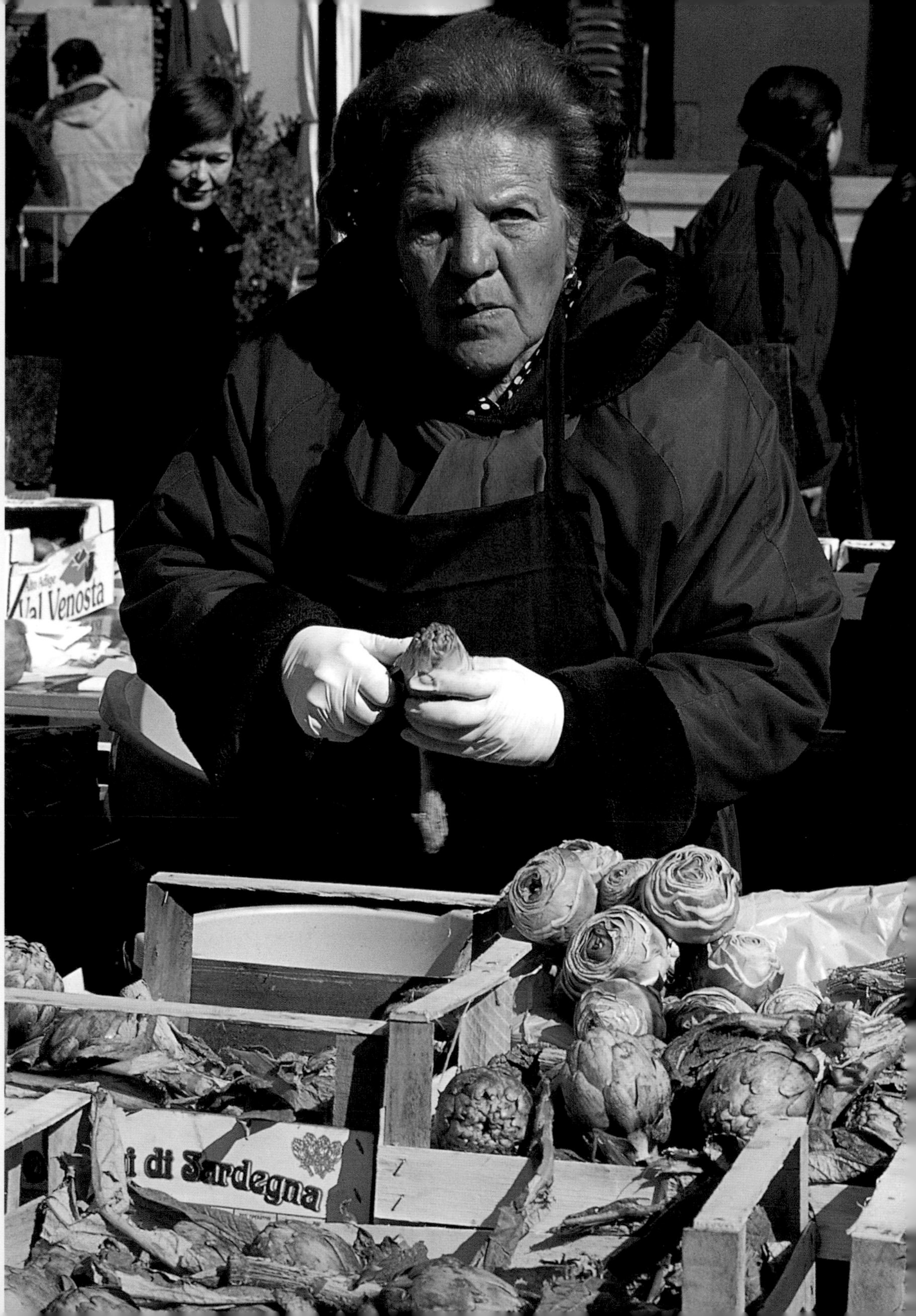
Val Venosta
di Sardegna

American-grown artichokes are too large and tough to be treated in this manner. *Carciofi alla giudia* must be made from small, tender, freshly picked artichokes. They are best eaten in Rome, preferably in or near the Jewish ghetto, where this dish was invented. The ambitious cook who has access to freshly picked artichokes of extraordinary flavor may find success in making them, if only they can once look over the shoulder of a practiced Roman cook to watch every deft cut and turn.

The artichoke recipes I have provided in the main section of this book are every bit as good as this celebrated dish, but a bit more practical for the home cook.

Broccoletti: These young, tender "baby broccoli," which are the pride and joy of the Roman fields, are gaining popularity in America. The best (and most passionate) instructions for cooking them are written by Professore Luigi Volpicelli in the preface to Vittorio Ragusa's cookbook *La vera cucina casareccia a Roma e nel Lazio:* "The problem is all in understanding it properly. Take off every leaf, even the smallest . . . wash every filament . . . when the water comes to a boil, add the salt and then throw in the *broccoletti.* One moment only, to render them 'al dente.' They have assumed the color of amethyst. Eat them like that, then, boiled, without any condiment. They have their own flavor, and there is no need for any other. Those who have eaten them once never forget them."

Broccoli di rapa, also known as *cime di rapa, bitter broccoli,* or broccoli rabe, is very typical of Roman cooking. Once, it wasn't easy to find outside of Italian neighborhoods, but despite its fairly recent popularity, still is often not cooked properly. Even respectable American cookbooks misinform about the proper way to cook broccoli rabe. To render its bitterness palatable, it must be first blanched in salted boiling water for 4 or 5 minutes before it can be tossed in a sauté pan with hot extra-virgin olive oil and garlic.

Celery *(sedano):* A local saying that demonstrates Latium's affection for celery is *"a ciccio di sellero,"* literally, "here's to the heart of the celery," meant as a hurrah for something having happened just at the right moment. Eating raw celery dipped in extra-virgin olive oil and sprinkled with a little salt and freshly ground pepper is a premeal and post-meal pasttime in Latium. Eaten this way, it is considered as much a digestive as it is an appetite stimulant. Besides its raw virtues, celery is ubiquitous as an ingredient in all kinds of dishes, from sauces to stews to vegetable side dishes.

Fava beans, or broad beans *(fave),* are indigenous to the Mediterranean, going back at least as far as the Bronze Age. They have long been a staple of Latium, where they have been prized for their nutritional properties. Their growing season is short, so they arrive in the markets in spring with a bit of fanfare. Eating raw fava beans and pecorino in tandem is a spring ritual. Cooked fresh fava beans have a mildly bitter, barnyard-y taste that, to my palate, is incomparable with other beans. The pod of the fava bean is some six inches long, and must be removed to get at the bean itself. The shelled bean has an outer layer that must also be removed. This is done by pinching the navel of the bean where it was once attached to the pod bed, then squeezing it from the opposite end in order to force it from the skin. The fresh beans are excellent when stewed with garlic and *guanciale* (or pancetta) in the Roman fashion, or braised with olive oil, onion, fresh artichoke hearts, baby peas, and perhaps tender beet greens in the provincial style (see Spring "Soup," page 115).

I have tried frozen fava beans, but found them useless. Dried fava beans are not a substitute for fresh fava beans. They must be soaked and boiled like all dried beans, then passed through a food mill to remove the skins. Once prepared in this fashion, they can be made into a lovely puréed soup with the addition of sautéed garlic or onion, extra-virgin olive oil, and plenty of freshly ground coarse black pepper. It should be noted that some people are genetically disposed to favism, a disease caused by eating raw fava

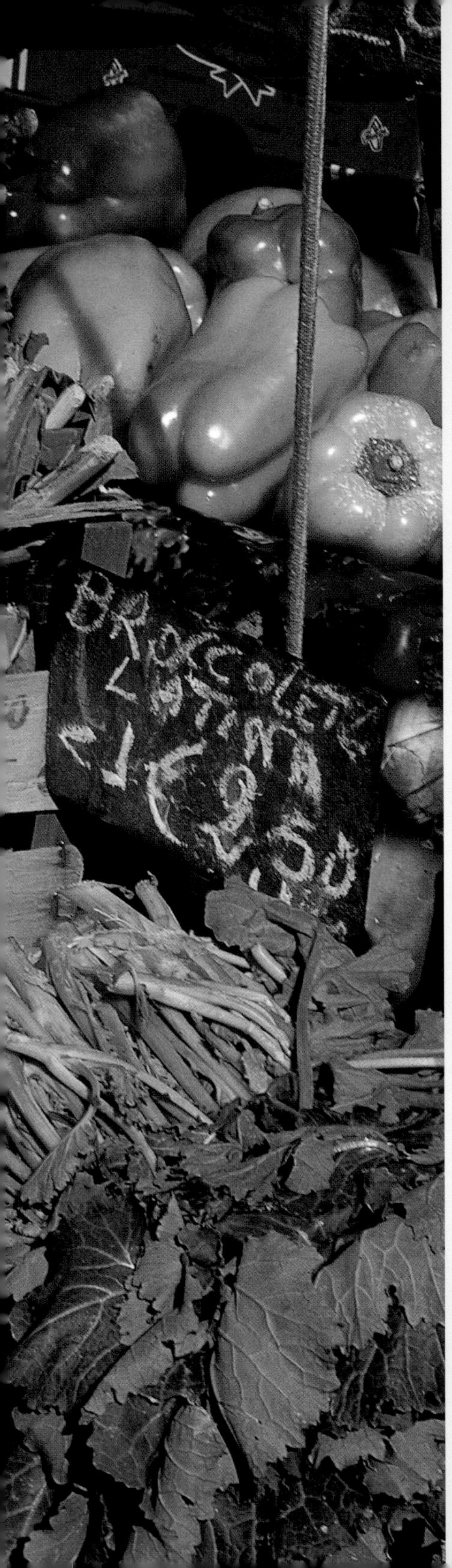

beans; the symptoms are those of an unpleasant allergy. However, the incidence of favism is rare.

Mint *(menta, mentuccia, e mentuccia romana):* An Italian publicity brochure about Roman cooking says that one has to have a refined nose and an educated palate to distinguish between these three varieties of mint. The first is peppermint, whose chemical attributes make it at once a stimulant, a sedative, and a calming influence on the stomach. *Mentuccia,* also called *nepitella,* is a wild mint of the same family that is foraged and sold at market. Its flowers are larger and more sparse than those of mint. Highly aromatic, its uncooked leaves are added to salads or used in cooking to flavor beans, meat stews, and vegetable dishes. *Mentuccia* was once thought to have miraculous healing properties, and Latium is still enamored with it. Roman *mentuccia* is an even more potent variety. *Mentuccia* is prized in other regions of Italy, but not as much as in Latium. Outside of Italy, other mint varieties can be substituted, including spearmint and peppermint.

Puntarelle (puntarelle di cicoria): Named after its pointed leaves, this green is also called Catalonia chicory or asparagus chicory. These long, crisp, pleasantly bitter winter greens appear from autumn through early spring. Their inner core is cut into long, thin strips, soaked in very cold water so it will curl, and tossed for a singular salad. *Puntarelle* has been known since Roman times, when Pliny wrote about its medical virtues and purgative properties. It is found throughout southern Italy, but is quintessentially Roman. *Puntarelle* salad is always dressed with extra-virgin olive oil, red wine vinegar, anchovy, and a generous amount of pepper. The outside leaves are often cooked like other greens: boiled and dressed with olive oil and lemon.

Roman lettuce *(lattuga romana):* Known to the English-speaking world as romaine lettuce, this plant has roots in ancient Roman soil. It is the lettuce Americans use for the ubiquitous Caesar salad, which has no relation to any Roman caesar, or to Roman cooking. It is said that the prospect of the planting season for this crisp, tasty lettuce caused the Roman legions to hurry home. In Lazio, it is the basic green salad when dressed with aromatic local extra-virgin olive oil and an excellent wine vinegar.

Walnuts *(noci)*

Walnut trees grow throughout Latium, especially in the Cimini Mountains of Viterbo Province. They were considered magical by the Romans, with both happy and sinister implications, and a symbol of marriage, reproduction, and prosperity. Pliny writes that the walnut tree is a guardian of strong marriages, for the two fast halves of the nut represent a steadfast couple. Both the Greeks and the Romans extracted a scented oil from the walnut. The nuts were used for many medicinal purposes, including an antidote for poison and, based on their resemblance to the brain, a remedy for psychological disorders. They are also used in cooking and baking, particularly as an ingredient in sweets. In Latium, as in other Italian regions, country people collect walnuts to make *nocino,* a sweet, potent liqueur. The recipe includes the fresh husk of the nut, cloves, cinnamon, lemon peel, sugar, and sometimes aniseed and rose petals infused in pure alcohol.

Noce e ppane pasto da sovrano.

Walnuts and bread: a king's meal.

—Roman saying

FACING PAGE:
"Broccoletti di Latina" or broccoli rabe from the southern coastal province of Lazio

LA CARBONARA

antipasti, svogliature e fritture

1 Appetizers, Snacks, and Fried Specialties

Left: Rome, Campo de' Fiori, panoramic view

Quer che appetisce nutrisce.

If it's appetizing, it's nourishing.

—Roman saying

Across Italy, the word *antipasto*, "before the meal," is used to describe the course that precedes the meal. The Romans use another word, *svogliature*. An Italian-English dictionary will not shed light on the matter, though *svogliato* means "listless, lazy." Should we imagine that the Roman is not yet hungry when he arrives at the table? It is pleasant to think of this "lazy" course where the Roman unwinds, eating many beguiling little dishes that will carry him or her over the threshold to dinner.

We can expect the course to include the local *prosciutti*, sausages, the olives, and other flavorful foods that, curiously, whet our appetites rather than calm them. Then there are the other *antipasti* specialties, about which I have written an entire book, *Antipasti: The Little Dishes of Italy*, that masquerade as appetizers, but can easily be main dishes in larger quantities. Rome offers more dishes in this category than does any other region, probably because it has always entertained larger crowds. In addition to the tasty *salumi* brought in from the Castelli Romani and surrounding provinces, these include a vast array of *bruschetta* (grilled fresh bread with toppings); marinated small fish perfumed with bay or other aromatics; olives stuffed with a meat and herb filling or scented with anise; an astonishing variety of bean, vegetable, and seafood salads; all kinds of inventions based on bread; and such specialties as the inimitable fresh raw favas eaten with pecorino, for which the whole region has an undying passion during its short, intense season. The brilliant flavors of the region's vegetables can make even the most seemingly banal dish taste astonishingly good. A simple appetizer along these lines was served to me in a little place directly on the shores of Lake Bolsena where I once stopped for lunch. It was nothing more than slices of wood-grilled juicy eggplant seasoned with local olive oil, chopped fresh parsley, and hot pepper. How delicious it was!

La fame è la mejo pietanza.

Hunger is the best dish.

—Roman saying

One category of appetizers that is obligatory in any discussion of Latian cooking, and of Roman appetizers in particular, is *fritture* or *fritto*, fried foods. The tradition of *fritture* in Rome's restaurants goes back to ancient times. There are a number of reasons for this. M. A. Levi, in his *Roma antica*, recounts that there was a certain tendency during the decadent period of imperial Rome to avoid, at all costs, the tiring mastication of foods (perhaps herein lies an explanation for the derivation of the mysterious *svogliature*). For this reason, tidbits of this and that were first deep-fried to make them tasty and crisp, then dipped into sauces. Another reason is the plain fact that the lower classes, which comprised the majority of ancient Romans, did not have stoves or ovens in their flimsy tenement buildings because they posed the danger of fire. Most eating was done in restaurants, or standing at stalls or carts on the street that offered everything from roasted sausages to the more affordable deep-fried vegetables and salt cod. The luxury of frying food in extra-virgin olive oil stopped with the fall of Rome. But, according to culinary writer Vittorio Ragusa, the taste for *le fritture* properly fried in olive oil returned at the end of the fifteenth century, when olive oil manufacture in Latium regained its vigor. In 1534, the French writer Rabelais, under the pseudonym Alcofribas Nasier, traveled to Rome and wrote *"Roma è tutta olezzante di fritti"*: "Rome is all filled with the perfume of *fritture*." Today, the typical Roman still dislikes the mess of deep-frying at home, so the restaurants where real Romans go fill in the gap, as they have always done.

"Bull's-Eye"

occhio di bue

FOR 4 TO 6 PEOPLE

about 1 cup extra-virgin olive oil

$^1/_4$ cup aged balsamic vinegar

sea salt for sprinkling

8 to 12 slices sturdy fresh bread, cut in half

Travel writer Mary Jane Cryan, an American who has lived in Viterbo for many years, writes about this snack, which comes into season with the olive oil harvest in November. The olives are pressed within twenty-four hours of picking, and everyone awaits the beautiful gold-green oil with anticipation because it is most delicious when new (olio novello)*. A favorite way to eat it besides drizzling it over bruschetta is to pour a small pool of it on a plate, then pour a smaller pool of balsamic vinegar in the middle. Add a pinch of salt and dip pieces of thick-crusted sturdy bread in it. The children call it* occhio di bue, *or bull's-eye.*

Distribute the olive oil evenly onto each serving plate. Carefully pour a proportionate amount of balsamic vinegar in the center of each pool. Sprinkle with salt to taste. Serve with the bread for dipping.

Black Olives and Celery Marinated with Herbs and Spices

olive "accondite"

FOR 6 PEOPLE

The black olives of Gaeta, in a zesty marinade.

1 teaspoon fennel seeds

1 teaspoon aniseeds

inner stalks of 1 head celery, including tender leaves, chopped

1 pound oil-packed black Gaeta olives

2 cloves garlic, crushed

pinch of red pepper flakes

2 teaspoons minced fresh oregano, or 1 teaspoon dried oregano

3 tablespoons extra-virgin olive oil, or to taste

1 teaspoon grated lemon zest

juice of $^1/_2$ lemon

In a small skillet over medium-low heat, warm the fennel seeds and aniseeds to release their oils, about 3 minutes, stirring once or twice.

In a serving bowl, combine the fennel seeds, aniseeds, and all the remaining ingredients. Toss. Serve at once, or refrigerate for several days.

Baked Eggplant with Meat and Pecorino Stuffing

melanzane imbottite

FOR 6 PEOPLE

3 small Italian eggplants, 8 to 10 ounces each

coarse salt for sprinkling, plus 1 teaspoon

6 tablespoons extra-virgin olive oil

1 red onion, quartered and thinly sliced

2 cloves garlic, minced

1/2 pound mixed ground pork, veal, and beef

2 slices stale bread, crusts removed

milk, stock, or water as needed to cover bread

1/2 cup chopped, peeled plum tomatoes

1/4 cup freshly grated pecorino cheese

3 tablespoons chopped fresh Italian parsley

freshly ground black pepper to taste

1/4 cup fresh bread crumbs

This is one of many ways eggplant is prepared in Latium. Use only Italian eggplants, which have a great deal more flavor than other types.

Cut the eggplants in half lengthwise. Make crisscross slashes about 1 inch deep in their flesh on the cut sides to facilitate hollowing out the eggplants. Use a large spoon to remove the flesh from each shell, leaving about ½ inch of the eggplant wall intact. Set the eggplant shells aside. Put the eggplant flesh in a colander and sprinkle generously with coarse salt. Put a dish on top of the eggplant in the colander, then top it with a heavy weight, such as a large can. Let stand for about 40 minutes.

Preheat the oven to 400° F. Rinse the salt off the eggplant, pushing out any excess seeds. Drain, pat dry, and chop.

Use 1 tablespoon of the olive oil to grease the eggplant shells inside and out. Arrange them, cut-side down, on a baking sheet. Bake until tender, about 20 minutes.

In a large skillet, heat 3 tablespoons of the olive oil over medium-low heat. Add the onion and garlic and sauté until the onion is translucent, about 6 minutes. Add the meat and sauté until lightly colored, about 3 minutes. Stir in the chopped eggplant flesh. Reduce heat to low and cook, partially covered, until the eggplant is tender, about 10 minutes. Remove the pan from the heat and let cool.

Put the bread in a small bowl and add the milk to cover. When it is soaked through, squeeze it dry. Add the bread, tomatoes, cheese, parsley, the 1 teaspoon salt, and pepper to the skillet. In a cup, mix together the remaining 2 tablespoons olive oil and the bread crumbs. Distribute the stuffing among the eggplant halves. Sprinkle some of the crumb mixture over each.

Bake until golden on top and cooked through, about 20 minutes. Let cool before serving. Or, make this a day or two in advance and reheat before serving.

Bruschetta with Mushroom Topping

bruschetta ai funghi

FOR 8 PEOPLE

This appetizer is made after meat has roasted for a second course, because a good deal of its flavor comes from meat drippings. The mushroom topping is offered on freshly grilled slices of bread.

10 ounces wild or cultivated mushrooms, or a combination

6 tablespoons extra-virgin olive oil, plus more for drizzling

1/4 cup dry white wine

2 tablespoons meat drippings

juice of 1/2 lemon

1 tablespoon chopped fresh Italian parsley

salt and freshly ground black pepper to taste

16 slices sturdy Italian-style country bread, grilled on both sides or toasted

Using a soft brush or a clean kitchen towel, remove any dirt from the mushrooms. Do not wash them because water alters their texture. Remove and discard any tough stems or woody parts. Cut the mushrooms into thin slices.

In a large skillet, heat 3 tablespoons of the olive oil over medium heat. Add the mushrooms and sauté until tender, about 8 minutes. Stir in the wine and cook until evaporated, about 1 minute. Stir in the meat drippings, lemon juice, and parsley. Season with salt and pepper.

Brush the bread with the remaining 3 tablespoons of olive oil. Spoon the topping on the bread slices, drizzle lightly with olive oil, and serve warm.

Pizza Stuffed with Broccoli Rabe from the Ciociaria

pizza con cime di rapa alla ciociara

FOR 8 PEOPLE

FOR THE FILLING:

$1^1/_2$ pounds broccoli rabe, cut into 2-inch pieces

4 tablespoons extra-virgin olive oil

pinch of red pepper flakes

6 large cloves garlic, minced

FOR THE DOUGH:

1 cake (10 grams) compressed yeast, or 1 envelope active dry yeast

$^1/_2$ cup warm (105° to 115° F) water

about 4 cups bread flour

$1^1/_2$ teaspoons salt

2 tablespoons extra-virgin olive oil, plus more as needed

fine cornmeal or semolina for sprinkling

1 large egg, slightly beaten

This recipe from the Ciociaria is for a type of calzone made when broccoli rabe is in season. This slightly bitter vegetable is known in Italian under many different names but most commonly as rapini *or* cime di rapa. *A variation is to cover the filling with a layer of thinly sliced or crumbled roasted sausage.*

To make the filling: Blanch the broccoli rabe in salted boiling water for 4 minutes. Drain immediately, rinse thoroughly, and set aside.

In a large skillet, combine the olive oil, red pepper flakes, and garlic and sauté over medium-low heat until softened, about 3 minutes. Add the broccoli rabe and stir. Cover and cook over medium-low heat for a minute or two until tender. Toss frequently to ensure even cooking. Using a slotted spoon, transfer the broccoli rabe to a plate and let cool.

To make the dough by hand: In a small bowl, combine the yeast and ¼ cup of the warm water. Let stand in a warm place for about 10 minutes, or until foamy. Sift 1 cup of the flour and the salt together into a large bowl. Make a well in the center. Add the remaining ¼ cup warm water and the 2 tablespoons olive oil to the yeast mixture and pour the liquid into the well.

Using a wooden spoon, gradually stir the flour into the liquid until the dough becomes too stiff to stir with the spoon. Using your hands, form the dough into a ball. On a lightly floured board, knead the dough for 8 to 10 minutes, or until silky and elastic, adding flour as necessary to keep it from sticking.

To make the dough in a food processor: In a small bowl, combine the yeast and ¼ cup of the warm water. Let stand in a warm place about 10 minutes, or until foamy.Combine the flour and salt in the processor and pulse to blend, about 30 seconds. Add the remaining ¼ cup warm water and the olive oil to the yeast mixture. Stir gently and pour into the processor. Process until a ball has formed, about 40 seconds.

continued

Pizza Stuffed with Broccoli Rabe from the Ciociaria

continued

Transfer the dough to a lightly floured board and knead until silky and elastic, 3 to 4 minutes.

Put the dough in a lightly oiled large bowl. Lightly brush the surface of the dough with oil. Stretch plastic wrap tightly across the bowl, covering it completely. Let the dough rise at room temperature until doubled, 1 to 2 hours. If the dough rises too quickly, punch it down and let it rise again.

Preheat the oven to 450° F with a baking stone inside. Sprinkle a baker's peel with cornmeal. If you don't have a baking stone and peel, sprinkle a baking sheet with cornmeal.

Punch down the dough and transfer it to a lightly floured board. Knead for several minutes, until elastic. Flatten the dough into two disks. Working from the center of each disk outward, press and stretch the dough to make a $\frac{1}{4}$- to $\frac{1}{2}$-inch-thick round. Turn the dough over several times as you stretch it to prevent it from shrinking back. Transfer the dough to the prepared baker's peel or baking sheet. Cover with kitchen towels and let rise for 30 minutes.

Brush the dough lightly with olive oil. Drain the broccoli rabe and spread it over half of the dough, leaving a 1-inch border. The filling should not be thicker than about $\frac{1}{2}$ inch. Pull the other half of the dough over the topping. Crimp well to seal. Using a fork, pierce the top of the pizza with plenty of holes. Brush the surface with the beaten egg. If using a baking stone, slide the pizza off the peel or baking sheet directly onto the stone. Otherwise, bake the pizza on the baking sheet. Bake until crust an even golden color, about 30 minutes. Remove from the oven and let stand for 5 minutes before cutting. Serve hot or warm.

Bread Salad

panzanella

FOR 4 PEOPLE

1/2 loaf (about 1 pound) 2- to 3-day-old sturdy country-style bread such as ciabatta or saltless Tuscan, crusts removed

6 tablespoons water, or more as needed

1/2 cup extra-virgin olive oil

3 tablespoons white wine vinegar

2 large vine-ripened tomatoes, or 4 vine-ripened plum tomatoes, seeded and diced

3 scallions, including 1 inch of the green part, thinly sliced

1/4 cup torn fresh mint leaves

1/2 teaspoon salt, or to taste

1/4 teaspoon freshly ground black pepper, or to taste

Tuscany, Umbria, and other areas of central and southern Italy all have their versions of bread salad. In Rome and Lazio, panzanella *is usually flavored with mint instead of basil. Use only sturdy country-style bread. Also essential is fruity, extra-virgin olive oil. This is a dish for summer, when vine-ripened tomatoes are available.*

Slice the bread and then tear or cut it into 1-inch pieces. You should have about 6 cups. Put in a shallow bowl and sprinkle evenly with the 6 tablespoons water. If the bread is very dry, add another 1 or 2 tablespoons water.

In a separate bowl, combine the olive oil, vinegar, tomatoes, scallions, and half of the mint. Stir and let stand for 10 minutes. Pour over the bread, add the remaining mint, and toss well. Season with salt and pepper and serve.

Make-Ahead Note: *Panzanella* can be made 1 or 2 hours in advance as long as a sturdy bread is used.

Tender Liver Sauté

"soffritto"

FOR 4 PEOPLE

12 ounces trimmed baby lamb's liver or calf's liver, partially frozen

1/4 cup extra-virgin olive oil

pinch of red pepper flakes, or to taste

sea salt to taste

1 onion, finely chopped

1/2 cup dry white wine

The popularity of baby lamb gives rise to a host of delicate and succulent dishes made from lamb's liver. Calf's liver can be cooked in the same way, with excellent results. Serve with bruschetta drizzled with extra-virgin olive oil.

Rinse the liver and pat dry. Slice very thinly. If using calf's liver, cut it into quarters, then cut into very thin vertical slices. In a large skillet, heat the olive oil with the red pepper flakes over high heat. Add the liver and sauté until nicely browned on both sides, about 4 minutes total. Season with salt and transfer to a warmed plate. Reduce heat to low, add the onion to the pan, and sauté until translucent, about 4 minutes. Stir in the wine and cook for about 2 minutes to evaporate the alcohol. Pour the sauce over the liver and serve at once.

Pan-Seared Stuffed Zucchini

zucchine ripiene

FOR 4 PEOPLE

4 young zucchini (about 8 ounces each)

1 slice stale bread, crust removed

milk, stock, or water as needed to cover bread

1/2 pound lean ground beef

1 egg, lightly beaten

1/4 cup freshly grated *parmigiano-reggiano* cheese

1/8 teaspoon freshly grated nutmeg

1/3 teaspoon sea salt

freshly ground black pepper to taste

3 tablespoons extra-virgin olive oil

3/4 cup tomato sauce

1/4 cup water

In Rome, stuffed zucchini are made with the whole small squash, which are cored, stuffed, and sautéed in olive oil, then cooked slowly in a little tomato sauce.

Using an apple corer or paring knife, core the zucchini, leaving about 1/4 inch of the zucchini wall and discarding the flesh. If it is difficult to core the zucchini, cut them in half horizontally to core, again leaving a 1/4 inch wall and discarding the flesh. Pat dry and set aside.

In a shallow bowl, soak the bread in milk to cover until it is thoroughly softened, about 10 minutes. Squeeze it well to remove the liquid and place it in a bowl with the meat, egg, cheese, nutmeg, salt, and pepper. Use your hands to combine all the ingredients.

Using your fingers, push the stuffing into the cavity of each zucchini. Form any leftover stuffing into small meatballs.

In a large skillet, heat the olive oil over medium-low heat. Add the stuffed zucchini and the little meatballs, if there are any, and sauté until they are nicely colored all over, about 12 minutes. If the pan is not large enough, sauté in two batches. Use tongs to turn them as they sauté to avoid puncturing them. Combine the tomato sauce and water and pour it into the skillet. Using a wooden spoon, stir to distribute the sauce evenly. Partially cover the skillet and cook over low heat until the zucchini are thoroughly tender and the filling is cooked through, about 10 minutes.

This dish is improved when made a day in advance. The stuffed zucchini can be reheated or served at room temperature.

Beans with Mussels

fagioli e cozze

FOR 4 OR 5 PEOPLE

$^3/_4$ cup dried cannellini or white navy beans, or $1^1/_2$ cups cannellini beans, rinsed

7 tablespoons extra-virgin olive oil

5 large cloves garlic, crushed but whole

2 pounds small or medium mussels, scrubbed and debearded

2 tablespoons white wine vinegar

$1^1/_2$ tablespoons chopped fresh Italian parsley

$1^1/_8$ teaspoons sea salt, or to taste

freshly ground black pepper to taste

This recipe was kindly provided by Villa Gambara in Bagnaia, Viterbo Province. Dried beans have better flavor than canned beans, but canned beans may be substituted as long as they are not very soft and disintegrated, as some canned beans are. The beans should be tender throughout, but not so soft that they break up and become separated from their skins.

Pick over the beans and discard any stones or any beans that are discolored or damaged. Put beans in a large bowl and add cold water to cover by 3 inches. Let stand at room temperature overnight. Drain them and rinse with cold water. Put them in a pot with cold water to cover by 3 inches. Bring to a boil, then reduce the heat to medium-low. Cover partially and simmer until tender but not falling apart, 35 minutes to 1 hour, depending on the freshness of the beans. Drain.

Or, put the beans in a pot with cold water to cover by 3 inches. Bring to a boil, then turn off the heat. Leave the beans in the hot water for about 1 hour. Drain, re-cover with water, and cook until tender. Drain.

In a large, heavy Dutch oven, heat 3 tablespoons of the olive oil with the garlic over medium-low heat. Sauté until the garlic is nicely colored, 2 or 3 minutes. Add the mussels and, using a wooden spoon, toss them to coat them with the oil. Cover tightly, raise the heat to medium-high, and bring to a boil. Reduce heat to medium and cook until the mussels have opened, 2 to 3 minutes. Remove from heat.

Discard any mussels that failed to open. Shell the remaining mussels and set them aside. You should have approximately 1 cup mussels.

Put the beans in a pan with boiling water to cover and simmer them for a minute or two, just to heat them through. Drain the beans well. In a medium bowl, toss the warm beans together with the warm mussels. Add the remaining 4 tablespoons olive oil, the vinegar, parsley, salt, and plenty of pepper. Serve warm.

Boiled Shrimp with Arugula

rucola con gamberetti

FOR 4 PEOPLE

1 pound large shrimp

juice of 1 lemon, or to taste

$^{1}/_{2}$ cup extra-virgin olive oil, or to taste

grated zest of 1 lemon

sea salt and freshly ground white or black pepper to taste

1 bunch arugula, stemmed

One afternoon my daughters and I had a nice lunch in a trattoria in the port of Gaeta. This was one of the simple appetizers we ordered, a lovely combination of shrimp and fresh arugula.

Cook the shrimp in boiling salted water just until they turn pink, about 2 minutes. Drain. Using a paring knife, remove their shells and the dark intestinal vein. Rinse quickly in warm water to wash off any traces of the intestinal matter and drain thoroughly.

In a bowl, combine the shrimp, half the lemon juice, half the olive oil, the lemon zest, and salt and pepper. In another bowl, toss the arugula with the remaining lemon juice and olive oil, and salt and pepper. Arrange a bed of dressed arugula on each salad plate. Distribute the shrimp evenly on top of the arugula. Serve immediately.

Batter-Fried Cauliflower

"pezzetti" di cavolfiore

FOR 6 PEOPLE

FOR THE BATTER:

2 eggs, separated

1/2 cup water

1/2 cup unbleached all-purpose flour

1 large head cauliflower (about 6 cups florets)

olive oil for frying

sea salt for sprinkling

Many of the beguiling fritture, *or fried appetizers, the Romans love so much—croquettes of various types,* supplì *(stuffed rice balls),* mozzarella in carrozza *(deep-fried mozzarella sandwiches),* provatura *(fried* provola *cheese) and the like—are treated to nothing more than a dusting of flour or bread crumbs before frying. Others are dipped in batter before deep-frying. The light and delicious batter-fried appetizers, called* pezzetti, *or "little pieces," can be of meat, seafood, vegetables, or fruits. Typical* pezzetti *include zucchini blossoms stuffed with fresh cheese, prawns, variety meats (calf brains, sweetbreads, and such), bite-sized pieces of cooked salt cod, broccoli, cardoons, artichoke hearts, zucchini, fennel, eggplant, and apples. Here we have cauliflower* pezzetti *the way Eleonora Paolucci makes them at La Chiesuola, her lovely bed-and-breakfast house in Bagnaia, Viterbo. The batter can be used for any of the foods just mentioned, but keep in mind that it must be partially prepared an hour or two before using. It may also be made in the morning and refrigerated, but the egg whites should be folded in just before using.*

To make the batter: In a medium bowl, mix the egg yolks and water together. Use a whisk to blend in the flour, but do not beat. Cover the bowl with plastic wrap and refrigerate for at least 2 hours or up to 8 hours. Keep the egg whites refrigerated.

One hour before serving, remove the egg whites from the refrigerator. In a large bowl, beat the egg whites until stiff, glossy peaks form. Fold the egg whites into the batter.

While the batter is resting, prepare the cauliflower. Remove the leaves and core and break it into florets of approximately equal size. Trim the stems if they are too long. Cook in a large pot of boiling salted water for 4 minutes. Alternatively, steam florets, and make up for the lack of salt with the salt shaker at the table. Drain the cauliflower well and blot with paper towels to dry thoroughly.

Line a platter with paper towels and place it near the stove. Pour 2½ inches of olive oil into a large, heavy skillet and heat to 375° F, or until a bit of batter dropped into the oil sizzles. Coat the florets with the batter, then carefully slip them into the hot oil. Do not crowd the pan, or the oil temperature will drop, causing the cauliflower to absorb excess oil. Cook until golden on both sides, turning once, about 8 minutes total. Using a skimmer, transfer one by one to the paper-lined platter to drain. Keep warm in a low oven while frying the rest.

Sprinkle with sea salt and serve immediately.

Grilled Provola Cheese

provola ai ferri

FOR 4 PEOPLE

1 tablespoon olive oil (optional)

about 1 pound "sweet" or smoked *provola*, cut into $^1/_4$-inch-thick slices

extra-virgin olive oil for coating

medium-coarse freshly ground black pepper to taste

This chapter ends as it begins, with the simplest of recipes, but one which, like the first, may be new to non-Roman cooks. Provola *is a mild, semi-soft egg-shaped cheese of Lazio (page 19), used extensively in cooking. Both smoked and unsmoked* provola *are prepared this way and offered as an antipasto, or even as a* secondo *in place of a meat dish. Other smoked and unsmoked semisoft cheeses may be substituted, including* scamorza.

Prepare a wood or charcoal fire in an outdoor grill, or preheat a broiler. Alternatively, heat the 1 tablespoon olive oil in a well-seasoned cast-iron skillet over medium heat. Using a pastry brush, coat the cheese slices on both sides with the extra-virgin olive oil. Cook the slices until the outside is seared and golden and the inside is runny, about 30 seconds on each side. Use a metal spatula to turn, and cook on the other side. Sprinkle with pepper and serve immediately.

primi piatti

First Courses of Soups, Pastas, Polenta, and Risotto

2

Left: Bolsena as seen when approached from the North

There is an obsession with soup and pasta in Rome and Latium, perhaps because once, when meat was scarce, the first course was often the only course. Leonido Vargas, writing during the nineteenth century about the cooking of his ancestors, describes it as "truculent, brutal, coarse, and flavorful." Many of these dishes, including some of the most humble, have survived.

Among typical soups is *acquacotta*, literally "cooked water," which is hailed a "dietic masterpiece among the single dishes of Tuscia" in a promotional pamphlet put out by the Viterbo chamber of commerce. *Acquacotta* shares its popularity with bordering Tuscany, which, like Viterbo, is resourceful with stale bread. There are an astonishing number of interpretations, but the soup always has four main ingredients: water, stale bread, greens (especially chicory), and extra-virgin olive oil. Hot red pepper is at the discretion of the cook. Although unrefined, *acquacotta* can be eaten with gusto, even today. The lake districts specialize in freshwater fish soups, and the coastal regions make *zuppa di pesce*, fish and shellfish chowders that derive their broth from wine, brine, and sometimes, tomatoes. The popular winter soups made with lentils, dried peas, or chickpeas have a long ancestry, proven by the frequency with which the ancients mentioned them in their writings. Others—to which I have had an aversion since I was a child but which nevertheless taste good to others—are of broth thickened with eggs. The most famous of these is *stracciatella* (a cousin to Chinese egg-drop soup).

Latians are also pasta eaters, a habit encouraged by neighboring Campania, the *maccheroni* capital of Italy. The ubiquity of dried pasta in its many different forms reflects the revolution that took place in nearby Naples during the 1800s, when advancements in technology made it possible to cheaply manufacture a type of pasta that could be dried, packaged, and stored for long periods of time. Also in the southern spirit, the tomato reigns, although unlike those of southern Italy, Latium's typical tomato sauces are meat based.

Sette cose fa la zuppa:
leva la fame e la sete tutta,
sciacqua er dente,
empie er ventre, fa smartire,
fa abbellire,
fa le guancie colorire.

Soup does seven things:
placates both hunger and thirst,
rinses out your mouth,
fills your belly, helps digestion,
makes you beautiful
and your cheeks rosy.

—Italian saying

Fresh pasta, the Etruscan legacy, is also prevalent. Ancient wall paintings and sarcophagi show cooks of Etruria making pasta and dressing it with olive oil, garlic, and hot peppers, as the Romans do today. Fettuccine, a descendant of the *laganica* of the ancient Romans, is a fresh egg pasta, the favorite fresh pasta of modern Romans. As Italian custom would have it, there is usually more than one name for the same thing, so there is much confusion as to what some local pastas are called. We find *stracci* and its diminutive, *straccetti*—"rags" and "little rags," respectively—which are different names for exactly the same pasta. The *maccarruni* of the Ciociaria are called *fini-fini* in other parts of the region. These are very fine noodles of white flour and egg yolks that resemble angel hair pasta. They are sauced with a tomato and chicken giblet sauce (page 66). *Lombrichelli,* or *ombrichelli,* long, thick eggless handmade strands, is identical to the *umbricelli* of Umbria, the *pici* or *pinci* of Tuscany, and the *bigoli* of Veneto. They also go by *brigoli, bighi, bichi, ghighi, tortoro, tortorelli, torcolacci, pisciarelli, visciarelli, filarelli, chicarelli, lilleri, scifulati, ciufulitti, cechi, ceriole, ciuci, spuntafusi, stratte, stringoli,* and *culitonni* in various dialects, all of which, according to an Italian food guide, are allusions to babies' penises.

I have included polenta in this chapter, although in Italy it is also served as a second course—or for that matter, as the only course. Corn polenta *(granturco,* or *mais)* made its way from the migrant farmworkers of Lombardy to the laborers in the Roman fields for the same reason that it gained so much ground in the poor regions of northern Italy: it was tasty, cheap, and filling. At first, it was considered poor food, and the humble people who ate it were disparagingly called *màgna-polenta,* "polenta eaters," by the wealthier classes. In time, it became diffused throughout the region and was eaten by rich and poor alike.

Farro and Cabbage Soup

zuppa di cavolo e farro

FOR 6 PEOPLE

6 tablespoons extra-virgin olive oil

4 cloves garlic, crushed

2 onions, quartered and thinly sliced

2 bay leaves

3 fresh rosemary sprigs, or 1 teaspoon crumbled dried rosemary

1 1/4 pounds cabbage, cored and shredded

4 plum tomatoes, peeled, seeded, and chopped

10 cups water

1 tablespoon coarse sea salt

1 cup *farro* berries (soaked in water to cover for 1 hour and drained) or coarsely ground *farro*

plenty of freshly ground black pepper

1/4 pound semisoft pecorino cheese, shaved into paper-thin slices

Although this is a meatless dish, the cabbage and onions provide a hearty flavor base. Cooked farro *berries or ground* farro *is used. Whole berries go nicely with the rustic character of the soup, but ground* farro *gives the soup a nice thick consistency.*

In a Dutch oven, heat the olive oil over low heat. Add the garlic, onions, bay leaves, and rosemary and sauté until the onions are translucent, about 6 minutes. Stir in the cabbage. Sauté until it softens, about 10 minutes. Stir in the tomatoes and sauté for an additional minute. Add the water and salt. Bring to a boil, then reduce the heat and simmer gently until all the flavors marry and the soup is fragrant, about 30 minutes. Stir in the soaked *farro*, if using, and cook the soup until the grains are tender but still somewhat chewy, about 15 minutes. If using ground *farro*, stir it into the soup during the last 10 minutes of cooking. Remove the bay leaves and rosemary, taste for salt, and add pepper. Ladle the soup into individual serving bowls. Cover the surface of each with a layer of pecorino shavings. Serve immediately.

Make-Ahead Note: As with any cabbage soup, the flavors are improved when it is made a day or two in advance. To cook in advance, make the soup, let it cool, then cover and refrigerate. When it is time to serve, reheat and add the pecorino to each bowl.

Lentil Soup with Sausage

minestra di lenticchie con salsiccia

FOR 6 PEOPLE

$1^1/_2$ cups brown lentils

10 cups water

1 tablespoon sea salt, or to taste

one 8-inch sprig fresh sage, or 2 bay leaves

3 tablespoons extra-virgin olive oil

5 links sweet Italian sausage, removed from casings and crumbled

4 cloves garlic, minced

1 onion, chopped

3 tablespoons chopped fresh Italian parsley

2 teaspoons fresh marjoram, or 1 teaspoon crumbled dried marjoram

1 cup tomato purée or tomato sauce

freshly ground black pepper to taste

One evening, my cousin, a member of parliament in Rome, took me to a casual trattoria on the second floor of an unassuming palazzo near the piazza Colonna, where the cabinet offices are located. The place was a noisy hub of politicians from all over Italy, and in it was to be found some of the best food in Rome. The waiters scurried about delivering a bewildering assortment of dishes to their discriminating clientele in the midst of the din. The food was as fresh and personal as the best home cooking—no doubt what all these weary parliamentarians wanted most when they were away from home. The lentil soup I ate there was probably the best I've tasted.

Pick over and rinse the lentils. Transfer them to a large pot and add the water, 1 tablespoon salt, and sage. Bring to a boil. Immediately reduce the heat and cook gently for 15 minutes.

In the meantime, in a large skillet, heat the olive oil over medium-low heat. Add the sausage and sauté until it is browned on the outside and still pink inside, about 8 minutes. Reduce the heat to low and stir in the garlic, onion, parsley, and marjoram. Sauté until the onion is translucent, about 4 minutes. Stir in the tomato purée. Add the sausage mixture to the lentils and mix well. Simmer for an additional 5 minutes to marry the flavors. Remove the sage, taste for salt, and season with pepper. Serve hot.

Pasta and Chickpeas

pasta e ceci

FOR 4 PEOPLE

2 cups dried chickpeas

1/2 teaspoon baking soda

1 large unpeeled clove garlic, plus 3 cloves garlic, minced

1 celery stalk with leaves

1 small branch fresh rosemary

7 cups water

2 teaspoons sea salt

3 tablespoons extra-virgin olive oil

4 ounces pancetta, cut into small dice

2 tablespoons tomato paste

4 ounces dried tagliatelle or other dried ribbon pasta, broken up

1/2 teaspoon freshly ground black pepper, or to taste

One of Rome's favorite humble dishes. Some versions include dried chestnuts.

Pick over and rinse the chickpeas. Put them in a bowl and add cold water to cover. Stir in the baking soda. Soak for 24 hours. Drain and rinse well.

In a soup pot, combine the chickpeas, the unpeeled garlic clove, the celery stalk, rosemary, and 7 cups water. Bring to a gentle boil, partially cover, and cook until tender, about 1 1/2 hours. Add the salt and let the chickpeas stand for 5 minutes to absorb it. Remove and discard the rosemary and celery. Remove 1 cup of the chickpeas and mash them. Return them to the pot.

In a medium skillet, heat the olive oil over medium-low heat and add the pancetta. Sauté until golden brown, about 3 minutes. Stir in the minced garlic, reduce the heat to low, and sauté until softened, about 1 minute. Add the tomato paste and 1/2 cup of broth from the chickpeas. Stir together and add the sautéed mixture to the soup pot with the chickpeas. Bring to a gentle boil and cook over medium heat for 10 minutes. Stir in the pasta and cook until it is not quite al dente, about 4 minutes. Check for salt and season with pepper. Ladle into individual soup bowls and serve.

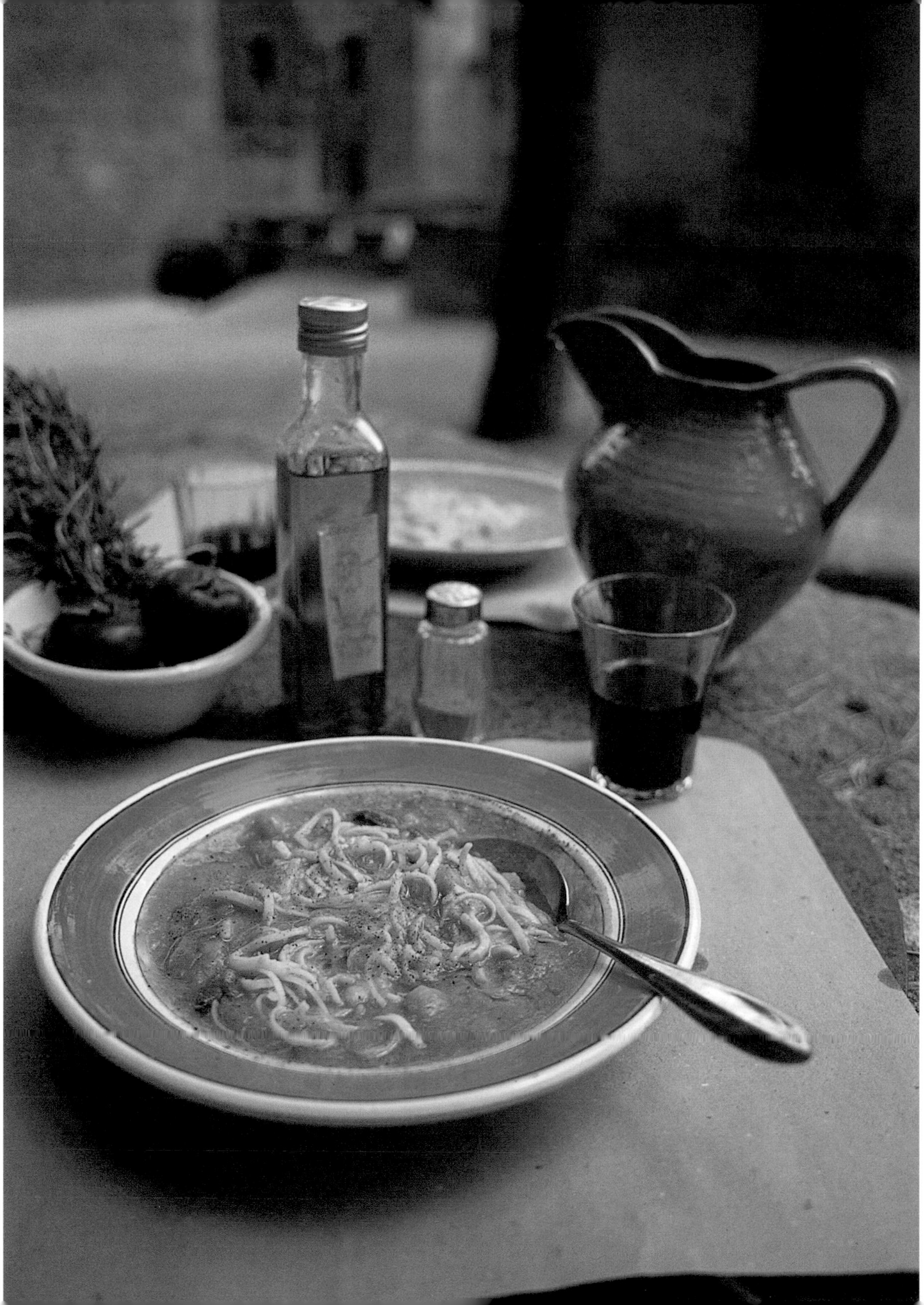

Spaghetti with Tomato and Bacon Sauce in the Style of Amatrice

spaghetti all'amatriciana

FOR 4 TO 6 PEOPLE

2 tablespoons extra-virgin olive oil

1/2 small onion, finely chopped

3 ounces lean pancetta, thickly sliced and julienned

1/8 teaspoon red pepper flakes, or to taste

2 tablespoons tomato paste

28 ounces canned Italian plum tomatoes in juice, drained (juices reserved), seeded, and chopped, or 2 1/2 pounds vine-ripened tomatoes, peeled, seeded, and chopped, juice reserved

1/2 teaspoon sea salt

2 tablespoons freshly grated aged pecorino romano, plus more for serving

1 pound imported Italian spaghetti

2 tablespoons coarse salt

This dish, which originated in Rieti Province, is one of Latium's best-known pasta specialties. The sauce is traditionally made with guanciale, *salted and cured pig's jowl, a specialty of the province and of Latium in general. Pancetta can be substituted. The method I have given involves adding grated pecorino in three stages, once during the cooking of the sauce, once when the pasta and sauce are tossed together in a skillet, and a last time when it is sprinkled on the served pasta. The idea is to deepen the flavor of the sauce and give it a voluptuous consistency. Credit for this innovation is due to the local master of* spaghetti all'amatriciana, *Livio Jannattoni (acccording to* Guida insolita del Lazio, *by Claudio Rendina).*

In a large skillet, warm the olive oil over medium-low heat. Add the onion and pancetta and sauté until golden, about 6 minutes. Do not allow the onion to brown. Stir in the red pepper flakes and the tomato paste. Add the tomatoes, their reserved juice, and the sea salt. Simmer, uncovered, over medium-low heat until thickened, about 30 minutes, stirring occasionally. Stir in 1 tablespoon of the pecorino. Remove the pan from the heat and keep warm.

Fill a large pot with 5 quarts of water. Bring it to a boil and add the pasta and the coarse salt together. Stir immediately. Cook over high heat, stirring occasionally to prevent the pasta from sticking together, until al dente, about 7 minutes.

Drain the pasta, add it to the sauce in the skillet, and toss well. Sprinkle in the second tablespoon of pecorino and toss again. When the strands are well coated with the sauce, immediately divide the pasta among serving plates. Serve more pecorino alongside.

Acquacotta ("Cooked Water") in the Style of Lazio

acquacotta laziale

FOR 4 PEOPLE

3 quarts water or vegetable or chicken broth

6 large cloves garlic, each cut into several pieces

1 small dried red pepper, or a pinch of red pepper flakes

1 onion, quartered and thinly sliced

1 pound flavorful tomatoes, peeled, seeded, and chopped, or 1 cup canned plum tomatoes, seeded and chopped

4 small potatoes, peeled and diced

1 small handful fresh basil leaves, torn into small pieces

salt to taste

1 pound curly endive, cut into small pieces

1 bunch arugula, cut into small pieces

8 slices stale sturdy country-style bread

8 tablespoons extra-virgin olive oil

8 tablespoons freshly grated pecorino cheese

The addition of vegetables, greens, and when available, erbarelle, *or wild herbs and field greens, provides enough flavor to make a tasty meatless broth. The greens might include wild chicory, young dandelion greens, wild cresses, valerian, wild chard, and potent wild mint. A successful* acquacotta *can also be made from a combination of commonly available vegetables and greens. An important part of the soup is the base of hard, sturdy country bread and richly flavored extra-virgin olive oil.*

In a soup pot, combine the water, garlic, red pepper, onion, tomatoes, potatoes, basil, and salt. Bring to a boil and simmer until the potatoes are nearly tender, about 10 minutes. Add the curly endive and arugula and simmer for another 5 minutes. The greens will be bulky until they have boiled and most of their liquid becomes part of the broth. Taste for salt.

Arrange 2 slices of bread in each serving bowl. Pour 2 tablespoons of the olive oil over each. Ladle the soup over the bread and sprinkle about 2 tablespoons of cheese over the top. Serve immediately.

Macaroni from Ciociaria with Tomato and Chicken Giblet Sauce

maccarruni ciociari

FOR 4 TO 6 PEOPLE

4 chicken livers

1/2 pound chicken giblets (gizzards and hearts)

5 tablespoons extra-virgin olive oil

2 cloves garlic, minced

1 onion, finely chopped

1 carrot, scraped and chopped

1 celery stalk with leaves, minced

three 6-inch sprigs fresh rosemary, tied with kitchen string, or 1/2 teaspoon crumbled dried rosemary

3 tablespoons tomato paste

1/2 cup dry red wine

28 ounces canned Italian plum tomatoes in juice, drained (juices reserved)

3/4 teaspoon sea salt, or to taste

freshly ground black pepper to taste

2 tablespoons coarse salt

1 pound fresh tagliolini

freshly grated pecorino cheese for garnish

This is the sauce that marries with maccarruni ciociari, *fine hand-cut noodles made with flour and egg yolks. Tagliolini, fine egg noodles, can be substituted. For the sauce, the chicken livers must be plump and firm. The best-tasting giblets are from free-range birds that have not been feed antibiotics, growth stimulants, or other unnatural additives. This sauce is also a good match for other types of pasta, including penne and other short, dried pastas, and a good condiment for polenta. For any of these combinations, pass freshly grated pecorino at the table.*

Rinse the livers and giblets. Remove any fat, membranes, green spots, or other discolorations. Blanch the livers in boiling water for 1 minute. Drain and immediately rinse in cold water. Cover and refrigerate the livers for 1 hour. Cut the giblets into small pieces and set them aside.

In a large, heavy saucepan, heat the olive oil over medium-low heat. Add the garlic, onion, carrot, celery, and rosemary. Sauté gently until the vegetables are softened, about 8 minutes, stirring occasionally. Add the giblets and sauté until they are nicely colored, about 5 minutes. Stir in the tomato paste and then the wine. Cook to evaporate the alcohol, about 3 minutes.

Pass the tomatoes through a food mill directly into the saucepan. Alternatively, push out excess seeds from the tomatoes using your thumb. Strain the tomato juices. Purée the tomatoes in a food processor (if the seeds are crushed in the blender, they will impart a bitter taste to the sauce). Transfer the tomatoes and their juices to the saucepan. Stir in the salt and pepper. Simmer, partially covered, over very gentle heat until the giblets are tender and the sauce is thick and aromatic, about 45 minutes.

Cut the chilled livers into small pieces and stir them into the sauce. Simmer for 4 minutes to heat the livers through, and then remove rosemary.

Bring 5 quarts of water to a rapid boil. Stir in the coarse salt and the pasta at the same time. Cook over high heat, stirring frequently, until the pasta rises to the surface, about 1 minute after the water returns to a boil. Drain immediately and transfer to a large serving bowl. Toss the pasta with the sauce. Serve. Pass the grated cheese at the table.

Avevano però abituato i ricchi alle "poppe di scrofa" e alle lingue di pappagallo "parlante," e quando scesero i barbari e Roma assunse l'aria di una preda di guerra, tutti, ricchi e poveri, dovettero scendere a patti con la fame. Tornarono a cibarsi così di quei piatti che erano statti cari ai pastori del Campidoglio e che nei secoli successivei sarebbero diventata la terza matrice della cucina locale: la tradizione culinaria schietta e robusta delle pastasciutte sabine, ciociare e viterbese.

The rich had become used to eating sow's breasts and the tongues of talking parrots. When the Barbarians descended and Rome assumed the aspect of a war victim, everyone had to come to terms with hunger, the rich and the poor alike. So they came back to the dishes that had been dear to the shepherds in the Campidoglio. Over the centuries these became the root of local cuisine: the sincere and robust culinary tradition of pastas from Sabina, Ciociaria and the Viterbo regions.

—The Romans

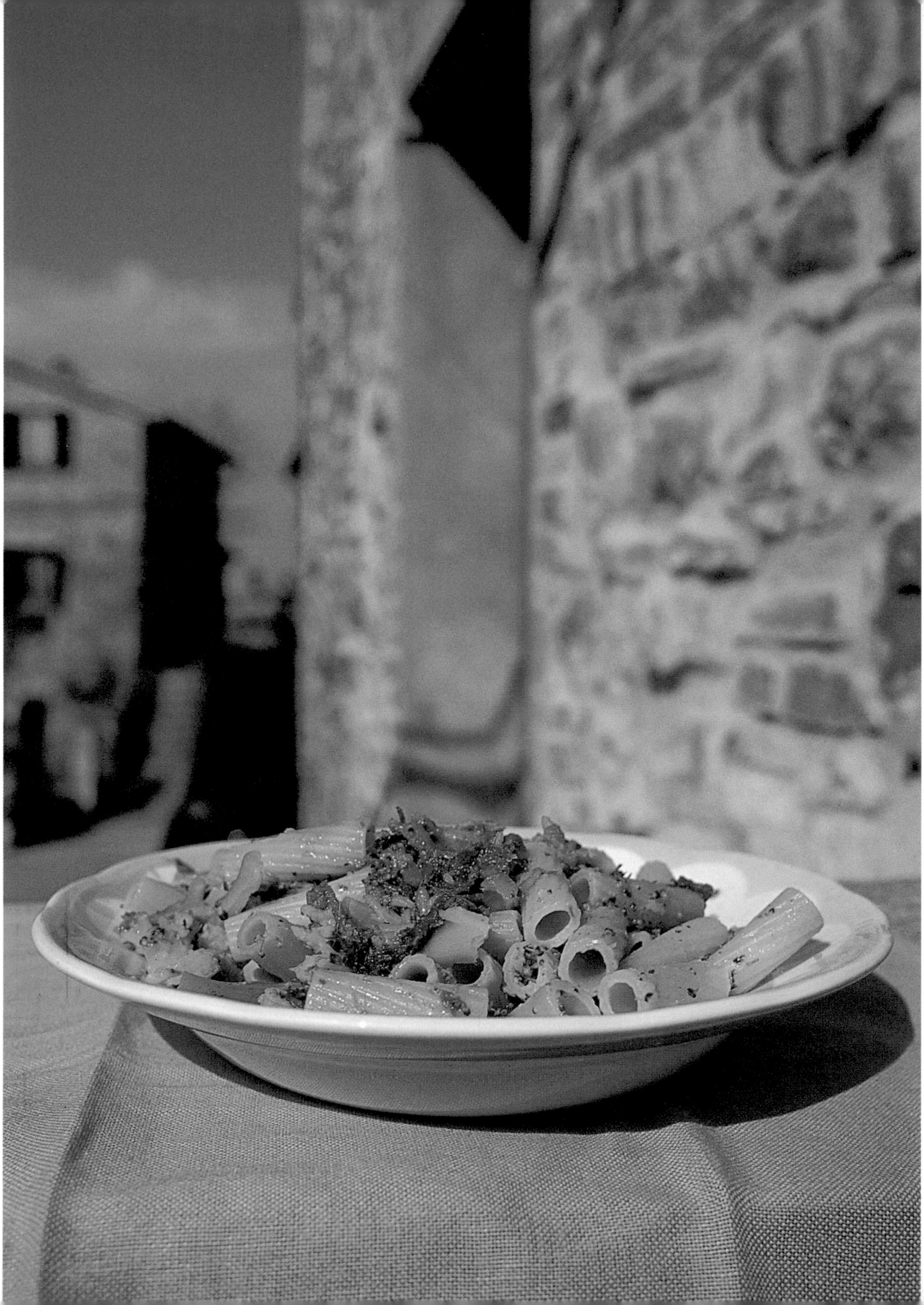

Rigatoni with Broccoli Sauce

rigatoni con salsa di broccoli

FOR 4 TO 6 PEOPLE

$1\frac{1}{2}$ pounds fresh broccoli

$\frac{1}{2}$ cup extra-virgin olive oil

1 clove garlic, minced

$1\frac{1}{2}$ cans (2 ounces each) oil-packed anchovy fillets

pinch of red pepper flakes

1 pound imported Italian rigatoni or ziti pasta

2 tablespoons coarse salt

My mother learned to make this dish when she lived in Rome as a girl. My sisters and I loved it, so she always made extra, but when it was time for second helpings, we still fought over who got more than the other. Even though my sisters thought they didn't like anchovies, they are an important part of this dish; the little fish dissolve in the hot olive oil that is tossed with the cooked pasta, leaving only a rich flavor.

Wash and trim the broccoli, removing any discolored leaves and tough parts on the stem. Separate the florets into bite-sized pieces. Cut and slice the stem into 1-inch pieces. In a small skillet, warm the olive oil and garlic over low heat. Add the $1\frac{1}{2}$ cans of anchovies and the oil from 1 can, then the pepper flakes. Cook until the anchovies are dissolved completely in the oil and the garlic is softened, about 3 minutes. Set aside and keep warm.

In a large pot, bring 5 quarts water to a rapid boil. Add the pasta, salt, and broccoli, and stir. Cook over high heat until the pasta is al dente and the broccoli is very soft, about 8 minutes. Stir occasionally to prevent the pasta from sticking together. Drain briefly (the pasta should still be dripping wet when tossed with the sauce) and transfer to a warmed bowl. Pour the anchovy sauce over the pasta and toss well. Do not serve with cheese.

Spaghetti with Tuna and Porcini Mushrooms

spaghetti alla carrettiera

FOR 4 TO 6 PEOPLE

$^1/_2$ ounce dried porcini mushrooms

$^1/_3$ cup hot water

$^1/_4$ cup extra-virgin olive oil

3 large cloves garlic, chopped

3 tablespoons chopped fresh Italian parsley

3 tablespoons tomato paste

28 ounces canned Italian plum tomatoes in juice, drained (juice reserved), seeded, and chopped

1 can (6 to 7 ounces) imported Italian oil-packed light-meat tuna, drained and flaked

$1^1/_4$ teaspoons salt

freshly ground black pepper to taste

1 pound imported Italian spaghetti

$1^1/_2$ tablespoons coarse salt

There are so many different recipes for spaghetti alla carrettiera *that it is impossible to figure out what the original ingredients were. One ingredient common to all versions is tomatoes. This recipe, purported by esteemed Italian culinary experts to be a genuine one, calls for canned tuna, but it's hard to imagine that the original did, considering its origins in the Alban Hills, so far from the sea. The dish originated with the* carrettieri, *the wine carters from the Castelli Romani who transported wine barrels to Rome in horse-driven carts. All recipes named for the* carrettieri *are very appetizing, and suitable for eating with plenty of white wine (particularly the wine made in the Castelli Romani).*

In a bowl, combine the dried mushrooms and hot water. Soak until the mushrooms are plump and tender, 20 to 40 minutes. Drain and squeeze the mushrooms over a bowl in order to reserve the liquid. Rinse the mushrooms under cold running water, then coarsely chop them. Set aside. Filter the mushroom soaking liquid through cheesecloth or a paper towel to remove any grit and set the liquid aside.

In a large skillet over low heat, combine the olive oil, garlic, and parsley. Sauté until the garlic softens without coloring, about 1 minute. Stir in the tomato paste and the mushroom liquid, then the tomatoes and their juices and the mushrooms. Simmer, uncovered, until the sauce thickens, 10 to 15 minutes. Add the tuna and $1^1/_4$ teaspoons salt. Simmer for another 5 minutes. Stir in the pepper and taste for seasoning. Set aside and keep warm.

Fill a large pot with 5 quarts of water. Bring it to a boil and add the pasta and coarse salt. Stir immediately. Cook over high heat, stirring occasionally to prevent the pasta from sticking together, until al dente, about 7 minutes. Drain and transfer to the skillet with the sauce. Toss well and serve at once. Do not serve with cheese.

"Green" Polenta

tardaglione

FOR 4 PEOPLE

3 tablespoons extra-virgin olive oil, plus more for drizzling

4 large cloves garlic, minced

pinch of red pepper flakes, or to taste

5 cups cold water, plus boiling water if necessary

8 ounces kale, stemmed and coarsely chopped

2 teaspoons salt

1 cup polenta

"Green" polenta is one of those fabled "poor" dishes that, like an old shoe, survived hard times and remained a favorite. It is a specialty of the mountainous Ciociaria territory. Vittoria Forte serves it in Ristorante Vittoria, her trattoria in Acquafondata, the highest town of the Meta Mountains. The "green" part of the polenta is a strongly flavored green called tanni *in the local dialect, for which there is no exact counterpart anywhere else, as far as I can tell. In appearance, its closest cousin is kale, but in flavor it is closer to broccoli rabe. Kale, collards, or mustard greens are the most suitable substitute. The greens are cooked directly in the polenta, thus "green polenta." Signora Forte advised that* polenta verde *is meant to be eaten* con cucchiaio *("with a spoon"), like a porridge.*

In a deep pot or large Dutch oven, warm the 3 tablespoons olive oil, garlic, and red pepper flakes over low heat until garlic is softened, about 2 minutes. Add the 5 cups water and increase the heat to high to bring to a boil. Stir in the kale and cook until nearly tender, about 7 minutes. Reduce the heat to medium and pour in the salt and polenta *a pioggia* (like rain), a little at a time, using a wooden spoon to stir well. Stir constantly, always in the same direction, in order to prevent lumps from forming and to keep the boiling temperature constant. This is important if the polenta is to become properly soft and creamy. The polenta is cooked when it is thick enough to resist stirring and pulls easily away from the sides of the pan, about 30 minutes. If the polenta is quite thick but still not pulling away from the pan, add a little boiling water and continue to stir until it is ready.

Spoon the polenta into serving bowls. Drizzle a little extra-virgin olive oil over each serving. Serve steaming hot.

Risotto with Puréed Asparagus and Smoked Provola

risotto agli asparagi con provola affumicata

FOR 4 PEOPLE

1 pound asparagus, tough stems removed lower part peeled

salt

about 3 cups hot chicken broth or mixed veal and chicken broth

4 tablespoons unsalted butter

2 tablespoons extra-virgin olive oil

1 leek, white part only, or 1 onion, finely chopped

2 tablespoons minced shallots

1 1/4 cups Vialone Nano, Carnaroli, or Arborio rice

2/3 cup dry white wine

1/2 cup freshly grated *parmigiano-reggiano* cheese, plus more for serving

4 ounces smoked *provola* or other smoked semisoft cheese, cut into very thin slices

freshly ground black pepper to taste

In Rome and Latium, rice is more often found in the form of risotto in restaurants than in home cooking. This is my adaptation of an outstanding risotto dish I ate in Rome during the asparagus season. The thin slices of smoked provola *(page 19), melted by the heat of the risotto, was a brilliant touch. Other smoked semi-soft cheeses (not mozzarella, because it is too stringy when heated) can be substituted.*

In a large skillet, bring enough water to cover the asparagus to a boil, add 1 teaspoon salt and the asparagus, and boil until tender, about 5 minutes. Remove the asparagus from the cooking water. Simmer the water to evaporate it to 1/2 cup and add it to the broth. Cut off the asparagus tips and set aside. In a food processor, purée the asparagus stalks until creamy.

Keep the broth warm in a saucepan over low heat. In a skillet, melt 2 tablespoons of the butter with the olive oil over low heat. Increase the heat to medium, add the leek and shallots and sauté until softened, about 5 minutes. Add the rice and sauté for several more minutes until the grains are opaque and click softly as you stir. Stir in the wine and cook until almost all the liquid has been absorbed. Stir in a ladleful of hot broth. Reduce the heat to low. When that liquid is nearly all absorbed into the rice, add another ladleful of hot broth. Continue in this manner, adding broth a ladleful at a time and permitting it to become absorbed before adding another ladleful of broth. Stir occasionally to prevent the rice from sticking to the pan. After the last ladleful of broth is added, stir in the asparagus purée. The rice should be tender but still slightly chewy, and the overall texture creamy and loose. Taste for salt. Remove from the heat, stir in the asparagus tips, the remaining 2 tablespoons butter, and the 1/2 cup *parmigiano-reggiano*.

Immediately divide the risotto among individual wide bowls. Distribute the *provola* over each serving. Serve piping hot, adding pepper as desired, and pass additional *parmigiano-reggiano* at the table.

secondi piatti di carne e pollo

3 Second Courses of Meat and Poultry

Left: Rome, Via del corso, man in ancient Roman costume advertises city tours

Alla trippa la menta,
al pisello il prosciutto e su tutt' e
due mettono un gotto.

Tripe demands mint,
peas demand prosciutto;
shower both with a glass of wine.

—Roman proverb

Romans like meat. This was adroitly put many years ago by a waiter in a Roman restaurant. It was a sultry August evening in the city, and I wanted a light dish. I studied the vast menu too long while our waiter stood ready to place the order. I asked for fish, but there were none on the list. "Signorina," the man said impatiently, "in Rome, we eat meat."

A look at any Roman menu, or any Roman cookbook, for that matter, will show that meat is preferred to any other food, even bread. Thus it is not surprising that the Romans are among the most discriminating at table of all Italians on the matter of meat. They like their meat very young, eating *maialino* (suckling pig), *capretto* (baby goat), and *agnellino* (milk-fed lamb), among other delicacies. These are, respectively, the tiniest of suckling pigs, the youngest of baby goats, and lamb butchered at a very tender age. Outside Rome, there are provincial preferences for other meats. In Viterbo Province the preferred meats are rabbit and fowl, spit-roasted lamb, and *porchetta,* as well as the usual variety meats. Mountain people raise sheep, so their preference is for lamb, as is the case in the Ciociaria and Sabine areas.

While their northerly neighbors, the Umbrians and the Tuscans, and their southerly neighbors, the Abruzzese, have a predilection for spit-roasted meats, the Latians and, in particular, the Romans, have a propensity for stews. This can be seen in the skill with which they transform economical cuts of meat into the most succulent dishes, including the family of *alla cacciatora* ("hunter's style") dishes (lamb *alla cacciatora,* chicken *alla cacciatora,* and turkey *alla cacciatora,* to name three), in which the usually ubiquitous tomato never appears, but where white wine or vinegar, garlic, rosemary, a touch of anchovy, and hot pepper invariably do. Nowhere else in Italy except for Venice and Sicily is there a predilection for the mingling of sweet and sour flavors. The Romans cook pork, boar, calf's tongue, and other meats

O fettuccine all'ovo benedette,
fatte cor sugo der garofolato, ch'é 'na
delizia poi, magnasse a fete!

Oh, blessed egg fettuccine,
smothered in the sauce of . . .
garofolato . . . meat, which is then
delicious eaten in big slices.

—Augusto Jandolo, Roman poet

in some surprising but tasty sauces that may include cloves, vinegar and sugar, bitter chocolate, pine nuts, and dried and candied fruit. One of the most famous of all Roman dishes is *coda alla vaccinara,* oxtail stewed in a rich ragù of herbs, golden raisins, pine nuts, or bitter chocolate. *Garofolato,* a thick stew of beef (in the Ciociaria, they use lamb or mutton) stuck with cloves and cooked with tomatoes, is a dish the Latians love so much that they write poetry about it. Not to be left unmentioned is the huge popularity of chicken and other fowl throughout the region, which no doubt has its roots in Etruscan cooking.

The other Latian propensity as far as meat goes is for innards, the cooking of which has been developed into an art form. The tradition goes back to times when only the wealthy classes could afford to eat meat, and the prime cuts were reserved for them. What was left over—the "fifth quarter" entrails, tripe, brains, liver, heart, tails, and hocks—went to the common people. No one in Italy makes innards taste as good as the Romans do, with the exception of the Venetians, with their brilliant treatment of liver, *fegato alla veneziana.*

Chicken with Tomatoes and Peppers

pollo alla romana

FOR 4 PEOPLE

$^3/_4$ cup all-purpose flour for dredging

$^1/_4$ teaspoon freshly ground black pepper, plus more to taste

$^1/_2$ cup extra-virgin olive oil

1 organic chicken (about 3 pounds), cut up (see headnote, page 66)

3 ounces pancetta, diced

2 large cloves garlic, chopped

1 onion, chopped

1 red and 1 yellow bell pepper, or 2 bell peppers of the same color, seeded, deribbed, and diced

$^1/_2$ cup dry white wine

2 cups seeded and chopped peeled plum tomatoes, drained (juice reserved)

1 teaspoon chopped fresh marjoram, or $^1/_2$ teaspoon dried marjoram

$^3/_4$ teaspoon sea salt, or to taste

$^1/_4$ cup water

This dish is named alla romana *because red and yellow are the colors of Rome. If both colors of bell peppers are not available, one or the other will do. There is plenty of thick sauce for serving with pasta, polenta (page 27), or potatoes.*

Put the flour on a sheet of waxed paper on your work surface. Mix in the $^1/_4$ teaspoon black pepper. In a large skillet, warm the olive oil over medium heat. Lightly flour only as many chicken pieces as will comfortably fit in the skillet at once and slip them into the pan. (If the skillet is not large enough to accommodate all the pieces at once, you will have to brown the chicken pieces in 2 batches.) Brown the pieces for about 5 minutes on each side. Transfer to a platter and set aside. Stir in the pancetta and sauté until it is golden, about 5 minutes. Reduce the heat to medium-low and add the garlic and onion. Sauté until the onion is softened and lightly colored, about 2 minutes. Add the peppers, reduce the heat to medium-low, and sauté until the bell peppers soften, about 8 minutes. Remove half of the mixture and reserve. Return the chicken to the pan and toss. Add the wine and cook for 3 minutes to allow the alcohol to evaporate. Add the tomatoes, marjoram, salt, and black pepper to taste. Stir in the water and bring to a boil. Reduce the heat to medium-low, partially cover, and simmer, stirring occasionally, until the sauce thickens enough to coat the spoon, about 40 minutes. Return the reserved bell pepper mixture to the pan during the last 5 minutes. Serve hot.

Eleonora's Hunter's-Style Chicken

pollo alla cacciatora di Eleonora

FOR 4 PEOPLE

1 organic chicken (about 3 pounds), cut up (see headnote, page 66)

3 tablespoons extra-virgin olive oil

1 onion, chopped

1/2 cup dry white wine

2/3 cup water

1/3 teaspoon sea salt, or to taste

1 large clove garlic, minced

2 oil-packed anchovy fillets, drained and chopped (optional)

4 fresh sage leaves, chopped, or 1/3 teapoon crumbled dried sage

leaves from 1 sprig fresh rosemary (about 1 teaspoon), or 1/2 teaspoon dried rosemary

2 tablespoons white wine vinegar

Given to me by Eleonora Paolucci of La Chiesuola in Bagnaia, this recipe for chicken alla cacciatora *is one of many permutations the dish takes throughout the region.*

Pat the chicken pieces dry. In a large skillet, warm the olive oil over medium-high heat. Add the chicken pieces and brown them lightly all over, about 15 minutes. Transfer to a plate. Drain the excess fat from the pan. Add the onion and sauté over medium-low heat until softened and lightly colored, 4 to 5 minutes. Add the wine and cook until the alcohol evaporates, about 2 minutes. Return the chicken pieces to the skillet and add the water and salt. Partially cover, reduce the heat to low, and continue to cook the chicken for 15 minutes, turning occasionally and stirring up any browned bits from the bottom of the pan. If necessary, add a little more water to the pan.

Meanwhile, in a mortar or a small food processor, combine the garlic, anchovies, sage, rosemary, and vinegar. Crush or purée all the ingredients. Add the mixture to the pan with the chicken and toss well. Cook the chicken over low heat until the breast pieces are opaque throughout, about 5 minutes. Remove the white meat parts. Continue to cook the dark meat about 5 minutes longer. Return all the white meat pieces to the pan and toss well with the sauce.

Serve hot.

Chicken Cooked with Vinegar

spezzatino de pollo all'aceto

FOR 4 PEOPLE

1 organic chicken (about 3 pounds), cut into small pieces (headnote, page 66), giblets reserved

5 tablespoons extra-virgin olive oil

3 large cloves garlic, chopped

3 small onions, chopped

6 tablespoons white wine vinegar

1/4 teaspoon freshly grated nutmeg

1/3 teaspoon ground cloves

1/3 teaspoon ground cinnamon

1 teaspoon grated lemon zest

1 teaspoon salt, or to taste

1/4 teaspoon freshly ground black pepper

1 cup water

Both chicken and turkey are succulent treated this way. If using turkey parts (legs and thighs), add the gizzards, heart, and liver of a chicken for added flavor. Whichever meat is used, have your butcher hack or saw it into manageable pieces for cooking and eating, like the Italians do. The breasts and thighs should be cut into 2 smaller pieces to prevent overcooking. Use a large, heavy knife to whack the drumsticks at the lower end to break the bone, making them flexible and easier to fit into the pan with the other pieces. The chopped giblets become part of the delicious and abundant sauce, which calls for plenty of bread to be served at the table.

Trim any tough membranes from the heart and gizzard and cut the meat into small pieces. Cut off any fat or membranes from the liver and cut it into small pieces.

In a large skillet, warm the olive oil over medium heat. Add the chicken and giblets and sauté to brown them all over, about 10 minutes. Transfer to a platter and set aside. Drain the excess oil and add the garlic and onions to the pan. Sauté over medium-low heat until the onions are softened, about 3 minutes. Add the vinegar and stir to scrape up the browned bits on the bottom of the pan. Stir in the nutmeg, cloves, cinnamon, lemon zest, salt,and pepper. Return the chicken to the pan. Add the water, partially cover, and cook until opaque throughout, 15 to 20 minutes, turning the pieces occasionally to ensure even cooking. Remove the breast pieces about 5 minutes before the dark meat.

Serve at once.

Roast Milk-Fed Baby Lamb

abbacchio al forno

FOR 8 PEOPLE

$^1/_2$ milk-fed baby lamb (15 to 20 pounds)

4 large cloves garlic, cut into slivers

$^1/_4$ cup extra-virgin olive oil

2 tablespoons minced fresh rosemary,
or 1 tablespoon dried rosemary

freshly ground black pepper to taste

sea salt to taste

The famous Roman abbacchio, *milk-fed baby lamb not older than six weeks, is almost as tender as butter when it is cooked. The best way to prepare this delicious meat is to do as little as possible to interfere with its natural flavor. The lamb needs no marinating, and no sauce save the pan juices. Have a butcher prepare the lamb for roasting. Be sure he cracks the joints so you can arrange the lamb on the rack on a roasting pan. Enough fat should remain on the lamb to keep it moist while it cooks.*

Remove the lamb from the refrigerator 1 hour before roasting. Preheat the oven to 400° F. With a small, sharp knife, make numerous small incisions on both sides of the lamb: in between the ribs, on the shoulder and legs, and between the joints. Slip garlic slivers into the cuts. Rub in the olive oil, rosemary, and pepper. Tie the legs together with kitchen string. Place the meat on a rack in a large roasting pan. Slide the pan onto the middle rack of the oven. Immediately lower the heat to 350° F. For "pink" lamb, roast 12 minutes per pound. After 30 minutes, remove the lamb from the oven and close the oven door (to keep the oven temperature constant). Baste the lamb with its own juices and return it to the oven. Repeat every 20 minutes.

Remove the lamb from the oven when the internal temperature of the thickest part of the meat reaches 130 ° F, and the surface is nicely browned, sprinkle with salt, and tent loosely with aluminum foil. Let rest for 15 to 20 minutes. Carve the meat and serve on a warmed platter with the degreased pan juices.

Braised Lamb with White Wine and Artichokes

abbacchio brodettato con i carciofi

FOR 4 PEOPLE

$^1/_2$ lemon

6 medium artichokes (about 6 ounces each), or 10 baby artichokes

2 pounds (trimmed weight) lamb shoulder or other stewing cut of lamb with some bone

3 tablespoons extra-virgin olive oil

3 large cloves garlic, crushed

1 carrot, scraped and shredded on the large holes of a box grater

$^3/_4$ teaspoon sea salt, or to taste

three 6-inch sprigs fresh dill

$^1/_2$ cup dry white wine

$1^1/_2$ cups water

freshly ground black pepper to taste

Given to me by my friend Clarisse Schiller, who lived in the Rieti Province for many years, this recipe is typical of the northern Sabine, where the cooking bears some similarity to that of the mountainous areas of bordering Umbria and Abruzzo. Delicate, pink-fleshed baby lamb is used, even for a stewed dish such as this one, but because it is difficult to get such young lamb outside of Italy, I have made some adjustments to the recipe, substituting stewing cuts. The artichokes, needless to say, should be fresh ones. Either fresh dill or wild fennel may be used. Once the artichokes are cleaned, the rest of the preparation is quite simple. This lovely stew is happy with good dry red wine at the table.

Add about 6 inches of water to a large glass or ceramic bowl (do not use metal), then squeeze the juice of the lemon into it. Trim a thin slice from the bottom of the stem of each artichoke. Pare off all the dark green skin on the stem. (The flesh of the stem is tasty.) With one hand, pull off the tough outer leaves until you reach leaves that have tender white areas at their base. Using a serrated knife, cut off the upper dark green part of the inner leaves; leave the light greenish yellow base. The inner rows of leaves are the tender part you want, so be careful not to cut away too much. (If you decide to use baby artichokes, keep in mind that they are more tender, thus there will be fewer tough outer leaves to remove.) Cut the artichoke in half lengthwise and, with a small knife, cut out the hairy choke and any other tough inner purple leaves. As each artichoke is finished, immediately put it in the lemon water to prevent it from turning brown. (Once cleaned, the artichokes can remain in the lemon water in the refrigerator for up to 24 hours.) When all of the artichokes have been trimmed, drain them, cut each half in half again, and pat dry. Cook the artichoke hearts in boiling water to cover for 10 minutes. Drain and set aside.

Trim the excess fat from the lamb, but leave the bones, which will add to the flavor of the stew. Cut the meat into bite-sized pieces. Rinse under cold running water and pat dry. In a large, heavy skillet or Dutch oven, warm the olive oil over medium heat and add the lamb pieces. Brown nicely all over, about 12 minutes. Add the garlic, carrot, salt, and dill. Stir in the wine. Cook to evaporate the alcohol, about 2 minutes. Partially cover, reduce heat to low, and cook, adding the 1½ cups water a little at a time, until the lamb is tender, about 1¼ hours, depending on the cut of the meat. Check the skillet frequently to prevent the meat from drying out. When the meat is almost done, add the artichoke hearts and cover. Cook over low heat until the artichoke hearts are tender and the flavors of all the ingredients marry, 10 to 15 minutes longer. Remove the dill and stir in the pepper. The thick, aromatic gravy calls for serving the stew with plenty of sturdy bread.

l'abbacchio è il più tenero del gregge, vergine d'erba, più di latte ripieno che di sangue . . . .

[Roman lamb] is the most tender of the flock, a virgin from grass, more full of milk than blood.

—Giovenale (Juvenal),
via *Le ricette regionali italiane (Recipes of the Italian Region)*

Stewed Baby Back Ribs and Sausages with Polenta

spuntature e salsicce in umido con polenta

FOR 6 PEOPLE

This Roman recipe was kindly given to me by Viola Buitoni. A dish of succulent pork ribs and sausages simmered in a dense tomato sauce is always served with polenta.

5 tablespoons extra-virgin olive oil

1 onion, finely chopped

1 carrot, peeled and finely chopped

3 celery stalks with leaves, finely chopped

3 sprigs fresh rosemary, or 1 teaspoon crumbled dried rosemary

18 baby back ribs, or 4 pounds "country-style" pork ribs (bone-in rib ends), cut off the rack into individual ribs

9 sweet Italian pork sausages, separated

1/2 cup dry red wine

5 cups (56 ounces) canned Italian plum tomatoes, drained (reserve juices), seeded, and chopped

salt to taste

FOR THE POLENTA:

7 cups cold water

2 cups polenta

1 tablespoon coarse salt

boiling water if needed

In a large, wide, and heavy copper pot or Dutch oven, warm the olive oil over medium heat. Add the onion, carrrot, celery, and rosemary, reduce the heat to medium-low, and sauté, stirring occasionally, until the vegetables are well softened, about 10 minutes. Add the ribs and sausages. Sauté until lightly browned all over, about 25 minutes. Stir frequently to prevent the vegetables from burning. Pour in the wine and stir to scrape up any browned bits from the bottom of the pan. Cook to evaporate the alcohol, about 3 minutes. Add the tomatoes, cover, and simmer, stirring occasionally, until the sauce is thick and the meat is so tender it falls off the bones, 2½ to 3 hours. Remove from the heat, remove rosemary, taste for salt, and cover to keep warm.

Thirty minutes before the meat is done, make the polenta: In a large saucepan, bring the water to a rapid boil over high heat. Add the polenta and salt. Reduce the heat to medium-low and, using a wooden spoon, stir constantly in the same direction to prevent lumps from forming and to keep the boiling temperature constant. This is important if the polenta is to become properly soft and creamy. Cook until it is so thick that it begins to resist stirring and pulls away easily from the sides of the pan, about 30 minutes. If the polenta is quite thick but still not pulling away easily from the pan, add a little boiling water and continue to stir until it is ready. Pour into a large serving platter alongside the stewed meat. Serve at once.

Adriana's Pork Loin Braised in Milk

maiale in brodetto all'Adriana

FOR 4 PEOPLE

$^1/_4$ cup extra-virgin olive oil

1 onion, chopped

1 clove garlic, bruised

$2^1/_4$ pounds boneless Boston butt

2 cups milk

1 sprig fresh rosemary

sea salt to taste

$^1/_4$ cup dry white wine

freshly ground black pepper to taste

Some years ago, a count I knew in Latium invited me to have dinner on his ancestral estate. He had a young pig slaughtered for the occasion, which his cook braised on the stove top. The meat was so delicious that I tried many times to reproduce the recipe. The results were always good, but the meat never reached the same succulence as the count's pig, which had been raised naturally, feeding on acorns and chestnuts. A Roman acquaintance, Adriana, recently provided me with her recipe for maiale in brodetto. *Although I have no choice but to resort to store-bought pork, the results reached the heights of flavor of the original.*

The gravy that is formed during cooking may appear to be somewhat curdled from the merging of milk and wine, but pan juices can be strained later for a smooth consistency. There will be enough sauce to cover a pound of tagliatelle, and certainly more than enough to moisten a side dish of potato purée. The meat should not be trimmed of excess fat before cooking, because it will add flavor and help to keep the roast moist during cooking.

In a large Dutch oven, warm the oil over medium-low heat. Add the onion and garlic and sauté until softened but not browned, about 4 minutes. Using a slotted spoon, transfer the onion and garlic to a dish. Slip the meat into the pot and brown it, turning frequently until nicely colored all over, about 15 minutes. Return the onion and garlic to the pan. Add the milk, rosemary, and salt. Cover and bring to a simmer. Reduce the heat as much as possible, using a heat deflector if necessary to cook it gently. Braise in this fashion, occasionally basting the meat with its own juices as it cooks, until tender, about $1^1/_2$ hours (or 25 minutes in a pressure cooker).

Remove from the heat, cover, and let rest for 15 minutes. Transfer the meat to a cutting board. Heat the liquid in the pot over medium-low heat and add the wine. Bring to a gentle boil, then remove from the heat. Remove the rosemary and strain the liquid through a sieve, pressing on the solids with the back of a large spoon. Season with salt and pepper to taste. Slice the meat and serve it with the delicious sauce.

Variation: Prunes or apples can be added to the pot during the last 20 minutes of cooking.

Veal Heart with Lemon and Parsley

cuore di vitello al limone

FOR 5 TO 6 PEOPLE

$1\frac{1}{2}$ pounds veal heart, partially frozen

2 tablespoons extra-virgin olive oil

1 large clove garlic, crushed

2 tablespoons chopped onion

scant $\frac{1}{2}$ teaspoon sea salt, or to taste

$\frac{1}{4}$ teaspoon freshly ground black pepper

grated zest of $\frac{1}{2}$ lemon

juice of 1 lemon

1 tablespoon chopped fresh Italian parsley

This is a dish from my childhood, one which my mother learned to make during the years she lived in Rome. She always served it with puréed potatoes, to top with the delicious and abundant sauce. It was always one of my favorites. It is a challenge to make nowadays when variety meats are so hard to find in the markets, but it is well worth the trouble of asking your butcher to order veal heart.

Trim all visible fat and tubes from the heart. Slice it into paper-thin strips 2 to 3 inches long and about $1\frac{1}{2}$ inches wide. In a large skillet, warm the olive oil over medium-low heat and add the garlic, pressing down on it with the back of a wooden spoon to release the juices. Sauté until golden and add the onion. Sauté until soft but not browned, 1 to 2 minutes. Increase the heat to medium, add the heart, and sauté until it loses all pinkness, about 5 minutes. Add the salt, pepper, lemon zest and lemon juice. Sauté for 2 to 3 minutes. Remove from the heat, sprinkle with parsley, and toss.

Note: The texture of heart is somewhat al dente—tender but firm—but the pan juices will keep the meat moist. For thicker gravy, remove the heart from the pan when it is cooked. Dissolve 1 tablespoon flour in $\frac{1}{4}$ cup cold water or stock and add it to the pan juices. Bring the liquid to a simmer, which will cause it to thicken quickly. Return the heart to the pan. Stir, sprinkle with parsley, and serve immediately.

"Jump-in-the-Mouth" Sautéed Veal Cutlets

saltimbocca alla romana

FOR 4 PEOPLE

1 pound (12 small slices) tender milk-fed veal scalloppine cutlets

12 large fresh sage leaves

12 thin slices (not paper-thin) prosciutto

5 tablespoons unsalted butter

2 tablespoons extra-virgin olive oil

sea salt and freshly ground white or black pepper to taste

2 tablespoons water

Saltimbocca, *meaning veal that "jumps in the mouth" because it is so tasty you can't wait to eat it, was invented in the city of Rome and is one of its most characteristic dishes. Outside Italy, this simple recipe is too often overwrought. The dish needs only tender milk-fed veal, authentic air-cured prosciutto, fresh sage, and good butter. It is critical not to overcook the veal.*

Place a piece of waxed paper on a cutting board and place a slice of veal on it. Cover the meat with another piece of waxed paper. Using the blunt side of a meat mallet, pound lightly on both sides to flatten and tenderize, being sure not to break the meat. To pound the reverse side, just flip the meat over, sandwiched between the sheets of waxed paper. Flatten all the slices very thinly in this fashion, replacing the waxed paper when necessary. Cut each slice into a piece no bigger than roughly 2 by 4 inches and discard the trimmed bits. You should have 12 thin scallop-pine. Place a leaf of sage on each slice, then add a slice of prosciutto the same size as the veal. Secure with a tooth-pick in the same fashion as you would place a straight pin in fabric to mark it.

In a large skillet, melt 2 tablespoons of the butter with half the olive oil over medium heat. Add half the veal, increase heat to high, and sauté until lightly golden on the bottom, 2 or 3 minutes. Season the meat with salt and pepper as it sautés. Turn the slices quickly to brown the other side for 2 minutes. Transfer the veal to a warmed dish. Add 2 more tablespoons of the butter and the remaining olive oil to the skillet and repeat to cook the remaining veal. When all the meat has cooked, add the remaining table-spoon butter and the water to the pan and stir. As soon as the butter melts, take it off the heat and pour it over the veal. Serve hot.

Note: *Saltimbocca* is often served with puréed potatoes.

Beef Stew with Cloves

garofolato di manzo

FOR 4 PEOPLE

$2^1/_4$ pounds flank steak, trimmed

1 cup dry red wine

1 small carrot, peeled and finely chopped

2 cloves garlic, finely chopped

1 small onion, finely chopped

1 inner celery stalk with leaves, finely chopped

2 tablespoons minced fresh Italian parsley

6 whole cloves

sea salt and freshly ground black pepper to taste

1 teaspoon minced fresh marjoram or $^1/_2$ teaspoon crumbled dried marjoram

2 ounces pancetta, sliced paper-thin

$^1/_4$ cup extra-virgin olive oil

1 tablespoon tomato paste

2 cups canned Italian plum tomatoes in purée, drained (purée reserved), seeded, and chopped

$^1/_8$ teaspoon freshly grated nutmeg

about 1 cup water

1 pound freshly cooked fettuccine for serving

FACING PAGE:
ROME, VIA METAURO DAILY MARKET, BUTCHER IN HIS STALL

Here is the most famous of all Roman stews, immortalized by a poet. Its name, garofolato, *comes from the cloves, or* chiodi di garofano, *with which the meat is studded.*

While the stew is cooking, fresh fettuccine is prepared. The first course is the pasta anointed with the delicious thick, aromatic gravy from the garofolato. *The meat follows as a separate course.*

Using a meat mallet, pound the meat to flatten it enough to roll easily. Place flat in a large, shallow baking dish. Pour the wine over the meat, cover the dish with plastic wrap, and refrigerate for at least 3 to 4 hours or as long as overnight. Turn the meat over halfway through the marinating period.

Remove the meat from the dish. Pour off and reserve the wine. In a small bowl, combine the carrot, garlic, onion, celery, and parsley. Lay the meat flat on a work surface. Insert the whole cloves evenly into one side of the meat, then sprinkle the meat very lightly with salt and pepper. Turn the meat over and rub ½ cup of the vegetable mixture over it. Sprinkle with the marjoram and lay the pancetta slices on top. Season very lightly with salt and pepper. Roll up the meat and tie it closed every 2 inches with kitchen twine. If necessary, use strong toothpicks to help close the meat. Set the meat roll aside.

In a large Dutch oven or other heavy pot, warm the olive oil over medium heat until it shimmers. Add the meat and brown it evenly on all sides, about 12 minutes. Transfer to a plate and set aside. Reduce the heat to medium-low, add the remaining vegetable mixture to the pan, partially cover, and cook until the vegetables are soft and lightly colored, about 10 minutes, stirring occasionally. Stir in the tomato paste. Return the meat and any juices that have collected on the plate to the pan. Add the reserved wine. Simmer, uncovered, to evaporate the alcohol, about 3 minutes, turning the meat in the pan to coat it evenly.

Add the tomatoes, their purée, and the nutmeg. Bring to a boil. Immediately reduce the heat to very low, partially cover, and simmer, stirring occasionally and turning the meat several times, 1 to 1½ hours, to ensure even cooking. Add some of the water at the beginning of cooking time to prevent the sauce from drying out. Stir in the remaining water as the liquids in the pan evaporate. In the end, a very dense sauce will result. If a thinner sauce is preferred, add a little more water. The *garofolato* is ready when the meat is thoroughly tender but not falling apart, and the sauce has thickened. Test the meat after 1 hour by inserting a sharp knife into the center.

Transfer the meat to a cutting board. Taste the sauce for salt and pepper. Remove the strings, any toothpicks, and the cloves from the meat. Loosely tent the meat with aluminum foil. Purée the sauce, ideally by passing it through a food mill. Otherwise, a food processor will have to do. (A food mill produces a sauce with a finer texture, as it strains out any fiber from the vegetables or tomato skins, if there are any. Puréeing in a food processor, on the other hand, results in a slightly thicker sauce, since it doesn't actually strain it.) Or, for a rustic sauce, serve as is.

Serve the sauce over the fettuccine. Slice and serve the meat as a second course.

4

secondi piatti di pesce

Second Courses of Fish and Shellfish

4

LEFT: STREET IN VENTOTENE, THE SECOND PONTINE ISLAND

It's not enough to buy the most costly species of fish at the tables of the fish market, if you then don't know what particular sauces should accompany them, nor the right way to roast them to make them appetizing to a guest who is already sated.

—Horace, *Satires, Book II*

The coastal areas of Latium live on seafood, just as the landlocked provinces live on meat. Likewise, the cooking traditions in the territories surrounding the three major lakes, Bolsena (the largest volcanic lake in Italy), Bracciano, and Vico, center around freshwater fish, and the lake dwellers are good at making them very tasty. In the Lake Bolsena area in particular, there is a cult of eel, a fish immortalized in Dante's Purgatory, where Pope Martin IV, among other gluttonous eel-eaters of infamy, burns under a torturous sprinkling of Vernaccia wine. In fact, the Vatican kitchen contained a tank where Bolsena eel could swim until they met their fate of being boiled in wine to be served on the papal plate. Eel are still stewed in white wine, including Vernaccia, or straightforwardly roasted, except at Christmastime, when they are given to special treatment. With the exception of some dishes from the Etruscan strongholds, particularly the Viterbo and Rieti Provinces, for the most part Latium derives its fish recipes from its bordering regions. Northern Latium tends to cook seafood the way the Tuscans do, and their freshwater fish the way the Umbrians do. Southern Latium, particularly the coastal stronghold of Terracina, where the biggest fish market in Italy is held every week, derives its inspiration for fish cookery from neighboring Naples. But the coastal towns of Gaeta and Formia do have an indigenous specialty, *sogliole gratinate,* crumb-coated roasted sole (page 105).

FACING PAGE:
Anchovy vendor, Gaeta's weekly market

Trout in Parchment in the Style of Lazio

trota al cartoccio

FOR 4 PEOPLE

2 tablespoons white wine vinegar

juice of 1 lemon

4 whole trout (1 pound each, they should be the same size and thickness)

BATTUTO:

1/4 cup extra-virgin olive oil

1 large onion, finely chopped

3 cloves garlic, minced

6 tablespoons minced fresh Italian parsley

extra-virgin olive oil for coating

sea salt and freshly ground black pepper to taste

As all of the flavor and moisture is sealed in a tightly closed packet, this method is an ideal way of cooking delicate fish like trout. Fish fillets can also be cooked this way, but keeping the fish whole allows the most flavorful parts—the head and the bones—to flavor the flesh of the fish as it cooks. Battuto *refers to the chopped aromatics inserted into the fish cavity. It is best to use fresh herbs, whose flavor and aroma permeate the fish without becoming embedded in the delicate flesh. An anchovy or two are usually stuffed into the cavity along with the onion and herbs, but I find this overpowering.*

Preheat the oven to 425° F.

Half fill a large bowl with very cold water. Add the vinegar and lemon juice. Add the trout and set aside.

In a small skillet, warm the olive oil over low heat and add the onion and garlic. Sauté until softened but not colored, about 3 minutes. Stir in the parsley and sauté until the onion is wilted, about 2 minutes. Remove from the heat.

Drain the fish and dry each one thoroughly inside and out. Cut 4 pieces of parchment paper, or foil, each large enough to wrap fish completely.

Coat the inside and outside of the fish with olive oil. Sprinkle the cavity and surface of the fish with salt and pepper. Spoon some of the *battuto* in the cavity of each fish.

Measure the height of each fish at its thickest part in order to calculate the correct cooking time. Place each fish in the center of a piece of parchment or foil and fold over the fish, folding the edges in several times to seal well. If using parchment, use paper clips to secure the folded edges. Place the fish packets in a large baking dish and bake for 10 minutes per each inch of thickness. Take care not to overcook. Remove from the oven.

If using parchment, each person can be served a fish packet on his or her plate at the table, but first remove the paper clips. If using foil, open the packet and transfer the fish to a serving dish or to individual plates. There will be plenty of natural juices to spoon over the fish after it has been properly skinned and boned at the table.

Freshwater Fish, Roman Style

pesce alla fiumarola

FOR 2 PEOPLE

1/4 cup extra-virgin olive oil

4 small freshwater eel fillets or catfish fillets, each weighing 4 ounces

2 bay leaves

4 cloves garlic, crushed

1 oil-packed anchovy fillet, drained and chopped (optional)

2 tablespoons small capers, drained, or large capers, drained and chopped

pinch of red pepper flakes

1/4 cup dry white wine

sea salt to taste

This is the way the lake people around Bracciano cook small river eel, ciriole. Fiume *means "river," thus* pesce *(fish)* alla fiumarola. *The flesh of the eel is delicate but firm, and will hold together even in fillet form when cooked. Catfish is a perfectly suitable substitute in this recipe. Anchovy fillets are often used to season freshwater fish in the lake districts because Rome and Latium love intense flavors, but I feel that they overpower the refined flavor of the fish, so I have listed anchovy as an optional ingredient. Bay leaf, also a typical flavoring for fish in the lake areas, imparts its lovely musky perfume ever so subtly, and red pepper flakes give the fish some fire.*

Dry the fillets well with paper towels. In a large skillet, preferably nonstick, warm the olive oil over medium heat until it sizzles. Add the fillets and sauté over medium heat until they are lightly colored on both sides, a total of about 5 minutes. Transfer to a dish and set aside. Drain all but 1 tablespoon oil from the skillet. Over medium-low heat, stir in the bay leaves, garlic, anchovy (if using), capers, and red pepper flakes. Stir to scrape up the browned bits from the bottom of the pan. Cover the pan and cook, stirring once or twice, pressing down on the garlic cloves to force their juices into the pan, until the garlic has colored nicely and the anchovy has disintegrated, about 2 minutes. Stir in the wine. Simmer until the alcohol evaporates, about 3 minutes. Return the fillets to the skillet. Cover, reduce heat to low, and cook until the fish is opaque throughout, no more than 5 minutes. Sprinkle with salt and serve at once. Remove the bay leaves before serving the fish, if desired.

Fish Fillets in Caper Sauce, Roman Style

pesce in salsa di capperi alla romana

FOR 2 PEOPLE

1 pound white-fleshed saltwater fish fillets, such as sea bass, sole, haddock, hake, or orange roughy

about 1/2 cup flour for dredging

freshly ground white or black pepper to taste

2 tablespoons unsalted butter

2 tablespoons extra-virgin olive oil

2 tablespoons small capers, drained

1/4 cup dry white wine

2 tablespoons chopped fresh Italian parsley

sea salt to taste

The Italians typically cook the whole fish rather than fillets, as the full, brinish flavors of fish are diminished when it is cooked without the head and skin. However, this sauce is so tasty that it will rescue even the most bland fish fillets, which are easier to find than whole fish in the markets these days. If increasing the recipe yield, sauté the fillets in batches to avoid overcrowding them in the skillet.

Pat the fillets dry with paper towels. This step is very important in order to sauté the fillets properly.

Place a large piece of waxed paper on your work surface and measure the flour onto it. Sprinkle with the pepper, then spread the flour out. In a large skillet, melt the butter with the oil over medium heat. Meanwhile, lightly dredge the fillets in the flour. Dredging must be done at the last minute to assure a crisp coating.

When the butter foam has subsided, slip the fillets into the skillet. Sauté over medium to medium-high heat until lightly golden, about 1 minute on each side depending on the thickness of the fillets, turning them only once. Transfer to a heated platter and reduce the heat to medium-low. Add the capers and wine. Stir to scrape up any browned bits from the bottom of the pan. Cook until the alcohol has evaporated, about 2 minutes. Stir in the parsley and salt.

Remove the pan from the heat and pour the sauce over the fish. Serve immediately.

Crumb-Coated Roasted Sole with Lemon and Garlic

sogliole gratinate

FOR 4 PEOPLE

- 1/3 cup extra-virgin olive oil, plus more for greasing baking sheets
- 4 whole sole (about 1 1/2 pounds each)
- 2 teaspoons fresh lemon juice
- 2 cloves garlic, minced
- 1/4 teaspoon sea salt, plus more to taste
- freshly ground white or black pepper to taste
- about 1/2 cup dried bread crumbs

Gaeta and Formia are known for this dish, one of the few fish specialties of Latium that didn't originate in Naples. While the Venetians believe that the only reason for adding lemon to fish is to disguise a foul smell, a bit of lemon juice sprinkled in the cavity along with olive oil and garlic is very pleasant. Sole is delicate, so just a touch of lemon and garlic is needed. This method is only for whole fish, not fillets, and it is successful with flounder and most other fish as well. Large fish can also be cooked this way.

Preheat the oven to 425° F. Grease 2 baking sheets with olive oil and slide them into the oven to preheat while you prepare the fish.

Using paper towels, pat the fish thoroughly dry.

In a small bowl, combine half the 1/3 cup olive oil, lemon juice, garlic, the 1/4 teaspoon salt, and pepper. Rub the mixture into the cavity of each fish. Rub the remaining olive oil over the outside of each fish.

Lay a sheet of waxed paper on a work surface and pour the bread crumbs onto the paper. Dredge the fish in the bread crumbs. Remove the preheated baking sheets from the oven and place them on the stove top. Arrange the fish on the baking sheets without touching each other. Measure the height of the fish at the thickest part.

Slide the baking sheets onto the middle and top racks of the oven and bake for 10 minutes per inch of thickness, or until the fish are opaque throughout when tested with a knife. If they require additional baking, return the fish to the oven at once, but be careful not to overcook them. Remove from the oven, transfer to warmed plates, season with salt and pepper, and serve at once.

Mariner's-Style Clams

vongole alla marinara

FOR 4 PEOPLE

4 dozen littleneck clams, or 4 pounds West Coast steamer clams or cockles

1 tablespoon coarse salt

extra-virgin olive oil for frying or drizzling, plus 3 tablespoons

8 slices sturdy French or Italian bread, crusts trimmed

1/4 cup water

4 cloves garlic, crushed

2 or 3 small dried red peppers, or red pepper flakes to taste

1/2 cup dry white wine

1/2 teaspoon sea salt, or to taste

1/4 cup or more chopped fresh Italian parsley

Some Roman versions of steamed clams are fiery with peperoncini, *hot red chiles. You can use as few or as many as you like. Clams from the Mediterranean are very small; many more than the two dozen littlenecks called for in this recipe would be used when making this dish in Rome. Cockles or the small West Coast clams called "steamers" (different from East Coast steamers) are closer in size to Italian clams.* Vongole alla marinara *is ladled over toasted slices of sturdy bread that have either been fried in extra-virgin olive oil or toasted and drizzled with it. Mussels can also be cooked this way.*

Put the clams in a large bowl of water with the coarse salt 1 hour before you are ready to cook them. Scrub them well under cold running water.

In a large skillet, heat 1/2 inch olive oil over medium heat until it is fragrant and fry the bread on each side until golden and crisp, about 8 minutes total. Or, toast the bread and drizzle each slice generously with olive oil. Put 2 slices of bread in the bottom of each of 4 shallow soup bowls.

In a large skillet with a tight-fitting cover, combine the salted water and clams. Add the 1/4 cup water to the pot, then add the clams. Cover tightly and place over high heat. Cook until the clams open, about 4 minutes. Transfer the clams to a large bowl. Discard any clams that have not opened. Pour the clam broth through a sieve lined with cheesecloth or a paper towel set over a bowl. Rinse the pot.

In the same pot, warm the 3 tablespoons olive oil with the garlic and red peppers over low heat until the garlic colors nicely, about 2 minutes; press on the cloves as they sauté to force their juices out. Add the reserved clam broth, wine, and sea salt. Bring to a boil over medium heat. Increase the heat to high. Add the clams to the pot and toss well. Cover tightly and cook, tossing frequently, until heated through, about 7 minutes. Remove from the heat, sprinkle with the parsley, and ladle the clams and their liquid over the bread in the bowls. Serve at once.

FARNESE
PELLICCERIA
DROGHERIA
UOVA
RAPSODIA IN
ASSO FRUTTA

5 Side Dishes

contorni

Left: Rome, Campo dei Fiori

Si dice che abbia virtù eccitanti e stimolanti e i gladiatori lo adoperavano come "doping" mescolandone i semi e le foglie agli alimententi.

It is said that fennel has stimulating qualities, and the gladiators ate it as "dope," mixing the seeds and the leaves with the stalks.

—Vittorio Ragusa,
La vera cucina casareccia a Roma e nel Lazio
(The Authentic Home Cooking of Rome and Latium)

Latium is very fond of vegetables. Nowhere else in Italy, for example, does raw fennel *(finocchio)*, dipped in olive oil and sprinkled with salt and pepper, hold its own as a single course. Or, consider the Roman passion for raw fava beans. Their brief growing season is eagerly anticipated, as well as that of wild hops (a relative of wild asparagus that the Venetians call *bruscandoli*), *puntarelle* (Catalan chicory hearts, page 32), and various wild greens and herbs. For the most part, the rest of Italy (except for the Piedmontese with their *bagna cauda*) considers eating raw vegetables crude.

Rome's famous and boisterous outdoor market, *Campo de' Fiori* ("the flowering field"), outdoes all the other markets of Italy with its mammoth maze of vegetable stalls. Whether due to the fiery Roman temperament; or to Roman vendors, who seem louder and shriller than those elsewhere; or to the perfect proportions of the Roman piazza, there is a greater profusion of fruits and vegetables, and their colors seem brighter than those in other markets.

With nearly half of its terrain covered with mountains, tufa rock, or parched stretches of earth and sand where only palm trees thrive, a good part of Latium is inhospitable to farming. But the fertile *agro romano*, the fields that surround the city, is intensely cultivated. Farther away, within an hour's drive from the center of Rome, is the Bolsena lake district, which sits inside a volcanic crater. The mild microclimate of the lake and the volcanic soil give rise to vegetables with exceptional flavor nearly year-round.

On the wild side, there are some dozen or so edible varieties of field mushrooms in Latium. Among these are the famed porcini *(Boletus edulis)*. Cicolano, in the Ciociaria, is such a poor area that it is becoming increasingly abandoned by its small population. But the one treasure it holds is the black truffle. A good example of Latium's utterly simple but profoundly tasty dishes is the region's favorite salad, *misticanza*. This salad of wild young greens and aromatic herbs originated with the Capuchin friars of the

Misticanza d'indiviola
D'erba noce e de ricetta,
caccialepre e lattughella
co' du foie de rughetta;
misticanza delicata
saporita e profumata.

Mesclun salad made of endive
walnut herb and curly leaf,
hare leaf and little lettuce,
with a pinch of arugula,
a delicate mesclun salad,
savory and fragrant.

—Augusto Jandolo, Roman poet,
as quoted by Vittorio Ragusa
La vera cucina casareccia a Roma e nel Lazio
(The Authentic Home Cooking of Rome and Latium)

region's monasteries, who foraged for the many tender, edible flora of the countryside they knew so well. We can only imagine what a genuine Capuchin *misticanza* would have brought together. No *misticanza* is considered authentic unless it contains at least eleven different types of greens, but borage, baby chicory, tender poppy flower leaves, and baby arugula are mandatory. The dressing is always the same: one part good wine vinegar and two parts optimal extra-virgin olive oil, put in the salad bowl in that order, and salt and pepper. The *misticanza* is added and all is tossed together.

Besides the brilliant flavor of the raw materials, another explanation for the imaginative range of Latium's vegetable cookery lies in the influence of, or better to say, restrictions of, religion. The Jewish ghetto (a stone's throw from the *Campo de' Fiori*) can take credit for many of Rome's exceptional vegetable dishes, the most famous of which is *carciofi alla giudia*. As well, the region's near total immersion in Catholicism since the eighth century bound the faithful to give up meat during one-third of the Christian calendar year. But the kind of self-deprivation practiced by the early Christians of Rome who traveled north to Ireland and elsewhere never took hold in Italy. A plethora of tasty vegetarian dishes were created in Italian kitchens, from monasteries to peasants' huts. The Italian sentiment in this regard was no better expressed than by Antonio Meneghetti, a former Roman Catholic priest turned philosopher, scientist, physicist, psychologist, artist, author, and gourmet, who planted roots in Scandriglia: "Good health is nothing more than being in harmony with nature.... It is important to seize pleasure, because we are nourished by pleasure. Virtue is nourished by pleasure; it isn't true that it is nourished by sacrifice." (*La cucina viva*, 1994).

Stewed Lentils

lenticchie in umido

FOR 3 TO 4 PEOPLE

1 cup dried brown lentils

1 bay leaf

2 teaspoons salt

1 celery stalk with leaves

1 carrot, peeled

1 small onion

1/4 cup extra-virgin olive oil, plus more for drizzling (optional)

1 large clove garlic, minced

1/2 cup tomato sauce

1 cup water or more as needed

Here is a popular dish that is eaten both as a side dish and as a main course with roasted pork sausages. It is always improved being made a day or two in advance.

Pick over and rinse the lentils. Cover them with cold water and soak for about 1 hour. Drain and rinse well with cold water. Put the lentils and bay leaf in a pot and add cold water to cover by 4 inches. Bring to a boil. Reduce the heat to a simmer and cook until not quite tender, about 20 minutes. Skim off any foam that forms at the top. Turn off the heat and stir in the salt; let stand for 5 to 10 minutes. Drain and set aside.

Finely chop the celery, carrot, and onion together. In a large skillet, warm the 1/4 cup olive oil and the garlic over medium-low heat until the garlic is nicely colored but not browned, about 2 minutes. Add the chopped vegetables, partially cover, and sauté, stirring occasionally, until softened, about 10 minutes. Stir in the lentils. Add the tomato sauce and 1 cup water to cover. Cover, reduce the heat to low, and simmer, stirring occasionally, until the lentils are tender, about 10 minutes. Add more water as necessary to keep the lentils from drying out; the consistency of the stew should be loose but not watery. Turn off the heat and let stand for about 10 minutes. Remove bay leaf, taste for salt, and serve. Drizzle a little extra-virgin olive oil over each serving for flavor, if desired.

Spring "Soup"

zuppa primavera

FOR 4 PEOPLE

1 lemon

5 baby artichokes

5 to 6 tablespoons extra-virgin olive oil

1 large onion, quartered and thinly sliced

2 ounces pancetta, finely diced (optional)

1 cup shelled fava beans

1 pound English peas, shelled (about 1 cup), or 1 cup frozen baby peas

1/2 teaspoon salt, or to taste

1 bunch young beet greens (about 3 cups), cut into ribbons (optional)

2 tablespoons chopped fresh Italian parsley

freshly ground black pepper to taste

My friend Clarisse Schiller lived for many years in the ancient town of Scandriglia in the province of Rieti. This is her recipe for one of the most anticipated spring dishes, also called scaffata. *It is not really a soup, but a delicious combination of braised vegetables.*

Add about 6 inches of water to a large glass or ceramic bowl (do not use metal), then squeeze the juice of the lemon into it. Trim a thin slice from the bottom of the stem of each artichoke. Pare off all the dark green skin on the stem. (The flesh of the stem is tasty.) With one hand, pull off the tough outer leaves until you reach leaves that have tender white areas at their base. Using a serrated knife, cut off the upper dark green part of the inner leaves; leave the light greenish yellow base. The inner rows of leaves are the tender part you want, so be careful not to cut away too much. When using baby artichokes, keep in mind that they are more tender, thus there will be fewer tough, outer leaves to remove. Cut the artichoke in half lengthwise and, with a small knife, cut out the hairy choke and any other tough, inner purple leaves. Cut the hearts into 8 wedges and immediately put them into the acidulated water to prevent them from turning brown. (Once cleaned, the artichokes can remain in the lemon water in the refrigerator for up to 24 hours.) Set aside.

In a large saucepan over medium-low heat, warm 5 tablespoons olive oil if using the pancetta, 6 tablespoons if not using it. When the oil is fragrant, add the onion. If using pancetta, stir it into the pan now and and sauté over low heat until the onion is translucent and softened, about 6 minutes. Drain the artichoke wedges and pat dry; add them to the pan along with the fava beans, peas, salt, and water to cover. Cover and cook over low heat for 15 minutes, stirring occasionally. If using beet greens, add them at this time. Cook for an additional 10 to 15 minutes, or until the artichokes are tender. Remove from the heat and stir in the parsley and pepper. Serve at once.

Stewed Fresh Fava Beans with Pancetta and Onions

fave fresche al guanciale

FOR 4 PEOPLE

1 pound fava beans, shelled

2 tablespoons extra-virgin olive oil

2 ounces pancetta, or salt pork, diced

1 small onion, finely chopped

$^1/_3$ teaspoon sea salt, or to taste

2 sprigs fresh mint

about 1 cup water

freshly ground black pepper to taste

This is one of Rome's classic fava bean dishes. Pancetta or salt pork can be substituted for guanciale, the favorite cooking fat of Latium. I remember my mother making this dish whenever she could find fresh favas in the market. The memory of the pork sizzling in the pot and the aroma of the beans stewing have stayed with me, probably because favas were such a treat on our New York table. The dish can be made only with fresh beans. Chopped fresh Italian parsley can be substituted for the mint. This is a good side dish with meat.

Blanch the beans in boiling salted water for 1 minute. Drain and rinse in cold water. Using your fingers, pinch the navel of each bean and pop it out of the skin.

In a large saucepan, warm the olive oil over medium-low heat until fragrant. Add the pancetta and sauté until lightly colored, about 3 minutes. Add the onion and sauté until it is nicely softened and the pancetta is lightly browned, about 4 minutes. Add the beans, salt, and 1 mint sprig. Stir in the water. Cover and cook, stirring occasionally, until the beans are tender and most of the liquid has evaporated, 20 to 25 minutes. If the beans begin to dry out and are still uncooked, add more water as necessary. Remove cooked mint, add pepper, and serve immediately, garnished with the remaining mint sprig.

Baked Artichoke Hearts with Garlic and Herbs

carciofi al forno

FOR 4 PEOPLE

juice of 1/2 lemon

10 baby artichokes, or 8 medium artichokes (about 6 ounces each)

2 cloves garlic, minced

1/4 cup chopped fresh Italian parsley

2 tablespoons chopped fresh mint

7 tablespoons lightly toasted bread crumbs

7 tablespoons extra-virgin olive oil

1/4 teaspoon salt

1/8 teaspoon freshly ground black or white pepper

3/4 cup water

The Romans are particularly fond of artichokes and probably have more ways of cooking them than just about anyone else. Tender young artichokes in season are used for this excellent dish, but larger artichokes will also do, as long as they are moist and fresh.

Add 6 inches of water to a large glass or ceramic bowl (do not use metal), and squeeze the juice of the lemon into it. Slice off the stem close to the leaf base of each artichoke. Trim a thin slice from the bottom of the stem and pare off all the dark green skin; slice the trimmed stem in half lengthwise and put it in the bowl with the water. (The stem is tasty.) Pull off the tough outer leaves of the artichoke until you reach leaves that have tender, white areas at their base. Using a serrated knife, cut off the upper dark green part of the inner leaves; leave the light greenish yellow base. The inner rows of leaves are the tender part you want, so be careful not to cut away too much. (If you decide to use baby artichokes, keep in mind that they are more tender, thus there will be fewer tough, outer leaves to remove.) Scrape out the hairy choke and any other tough, inner purple leaves. Put the artichoke hearts into the acidulated water to prevent them from turning brown. (Once cleaned, the artichokes can remain in the lemon water in the refrigerator for up to 24 hours.)

Preheat the oven to 375° F. Select a baking dish in which all the artichokes will fit snugly. In a bowl, combine the garlic, parsley, mint, bread crumbs, 5 tablespoons of the olive oil, salt, and pepper. Use a teaspoon to fill each artichoke bottom with the filling. Place the artichoke bottoms and the stems in the baking dish. Pour in the water and the remaining 2 tablespoons olive oil. Cover tightly with aluminum foil. Bake until tender, about 40 minutes. Check occasionally and add a little more water if the dish gets dry.

Remove from the oven and serve warm.

Make-Ahead Note: This dish can be prepared up to 3 days before baking.

Baby Peas Coddled in Lettuce

piselli alla lattuga

FOR 4 PEOPLE

In this adaptation of a recipe from Theodora Fitzgibbon's cookbook, A Taste of Rome, *I add fresh mint to the peas while they cook and season them after cooking with white pepper. The modern Romans are fond of peas, which are typically cooked with prosciutto or mint.*

8 large (outer) tender red leaf or Boston lettuce leaves

4 pounds English peas, shelled (about 4 cups), or two 10-ounce packages frozen baby peas

3 to 4 tablespoons unsalted butter, melted

1/4 teaspoon sugar

1/2 teaspoon salt

3 scallions, including 2 inches of the green part, finely chopped

1 sprig fresh mint (about 8 leaves), plus small sprigs for garnish

3/4 cup water

freshly ground white pepper to taste

Line a large saucepan with the lettuce leaves so that the botton and sides are covered. In a bowl, toss the peas with the butter, sugar, salt, and scallions. Transfer the mixture to the prepared pan. Add the mint sprig and water. Place another lettuce leaf over the top of the peas and cover the pan tightly. Cook over low heat until the peas are tender, about 8 minutes. Remove the mint. Serve hot, seasoned lightly with pepper and garnished with mint sprigs.

Peas Stewed with Prosciutto and Mint

piselli al prosciutto

FOR 4 PEOPLE

4 tablespoons extra-virgin olive oil

1 small onion, finely chopped

2 ounces prosciutto in 1 thick slice, cut into fine dice

4 pounds English peas, shelled (about 4 cups), or two 10-ounce packages frozen baby peas

1 tablespoon chopped fresh mint

1/2 cup water or chicken broth

salt and freshly ground white or black pepper to taste

While parsley is often combined with peas in other regions, the Romans favor mint. Fresh English peas are not easily come by, as their season is short and their sweetness and flavor perish quickly after picking. Frozen baby peas can be substituted with good results.

In a medium saucepan, warm the olive oil over medium-low heat. Add the onion and increase the heat to medium. Sauté until the onion is soft but not colored, 4 to 5 minutes. Stir in the prosciutto and sauté for 1 to 2 minutes. Add the peas and mint. Stir in the water. Cover and cook, stirring occasionally, until the peas are tender and most of the liquid is evaporated, about 15 minutes.

Add salt and pepper and serve immediately.

Roasted Onions with Vinegar Dressing

cipolle al forno

FOR 4 PEOPLE

6 onions, peeled

extra-virgin olive oil for brushing

sea salt to taste

white wine vinegar for sprinkling

freshly ground black pepper to taste

The people of Latium love onions, so much so that they consume one-quarter to one-fifth of the country's production. Latina is a particular stronghold of onion eaters. Writing in 1884, Oreste Raggi says that in the town of Marino, "everyone has to have their onions: for those poor people deprived of land to cultivate, the Comune [municipality] assigns a vast area of land for them called 'il Cipollaro' [the onion field]." Any type of onion can be roasted for this recipe, including the common yellow onion. Fresh onions of the season give best results. This is a good side dish for meat, fowl, or fish—or, in the style of Marino, it may be served as a main course.

Cut the onions in half crosswise. Place them in a bowl and add cold water to cover. Let stand for about 1 hour. Drain and pat dry.

Preheat the oven to 350° F. Line a baking sheet with heavy-duty aluminum foil and coat with oil. Brush the onion halves all over with olive oil and place them on the prepared pan. Sprinkle with salt and roast until thoroughly tender and nicely browned, about 1 hour. Transfer to a serving dish. Sprinkle lightly with vinegar and generously with pepper to serve.

Wild Mushrooms in the Style of Trastevere

funghi alla trasteverina

FOR 4 PEOPLE

10 ounces wild and/or cultivated mushrooms

5 tablespoons extra-virgin olive oil

1 small onion, quartered and thinly sliced

1 clove garlic, minced

2 tablespoons white wine vinegar

1 pound plum tomatoes, peeled, seeded, and coarsely chopped, or 1 cup canned Italian plum tomatoes, drained, seeded, and chopped

1 small bay leaf

1 tablespoon chopped fresh Italian parsley

1 teaspoon chopped fresh thyme, or 1/4 teaspoon crumbled dried thyme

1/4 teaspoon salt, or to taste

freshly ground black pepper to taste

In Trastevere, beautiful porcini are used for this dish when in season, but a combination of other wild mushrooms can also be cooked in this way. Try a combination: oyster mushrooms, or other wild varieties—even cultivated ones, such as shiitakes, will do. Serve at room temperature, or chilled as a side dish with roasted meats.

Using a soft brush or clean kitchen towel, remove any dirt from the mushrooms. Do not wash them because water alters their texture. Remove and discard any tough stems or woody parts. If they are large, cut them into halves or quarters. Slice the mushrooms thinly.

In a large skillet, warm 3 tablespoons of the olive oil over medium heat. Add the mushrooms and sauté until tender, about 8 minutes. In another skillet, heat the remaining 2 tablespoons olive oil. Reduce the heat to medium-low, add the onion and garlic, and sauté until softened, about 2 minutes. Stir in the vinegar and cook to evaporate, about 2 minutes. Add the tomatoes, bay leaf, parsley, thyme, salt, and pepper. Cook until thickened, 10 to 15 minutes. Remove the bay leaf and stir in the mushrooms. Let cool to room temperature, or refrigerate until chilled and serve cold.

Sautéed Spinach with Garlic and Red Pepper

spinaci alla laziale

FOR 2 PEOPLE

1 pound fresh spinach, well washed and stemmed

3 tablespoons extra-virgin olive oil or unsalted butter

1 clove garlic, minced

pinch of red pepper flakes

sea salt to taste

In northern Lazio, where there is a particular penchant for fiery foods, spinach is sautéed with extra-virgin olive oil, garlic, and red pepper. Escarole and other greens may be cooked the same way.

Drain but do not dry the spinach leaves.

In a large skillet, heat the olive oil with the garlic and red pepper flakes over medium-low heat. Sauté until the garlic is softened but not browned, about 1 minute. Increase the heat to medium-high and immediately add the spinach. Toss quickly and sauté, stirring often, until the spinach is completely wilted, about 4 minutes. Remove from the heat. Drain off excess liquid if you prefer, but keep in mind that it contains beneficial vitamins. Add salt and serve.

Boiled Potatoes Dressed with Olive Oil, Parsley, and Celery

insalata di patate alla Sbarra

FOR 4 PEOPLE

$1^1/_2$ pounds boiling potatoes, scrubbed

$^1/_4$ cup extra-virgin olive oil, or to taste

$^1/_4$ cup chopped fresh Italian parsley

tender inner stalks of 1 head celery, with leaves, chopped

sea salt and freshly ground black pepper to taste

The potato, introduced to Latium in the last half of the eighteenth century, has become a prominent part of the region's cuisine. It is almost always cooked with olive oil, as in this hot potato salad. The heat from the potatoes brings out the lovely flavor of the extra-virgin olive oil. Capers are often added to the dressing, but I like this version with celery hearts, which was on the menu at a terrific trattoria called La Sbarra in Acquapendente, near Lake Bolsena. Only flavorful, high-quality extra-virgin olive oil should be used in a dish like this consisting of only a few ingredients.

Put the potatoes in a large saucepan and add water to cover. Bring to a boil over high heat, reduce heat to medium, and cook until tender, about 20 minutes, depending on the age of the potatoes. Don't overcook them. Drain and let cool to the touch. Peel and cut into bite-sized pieces. While the potatoes are warm, toss them with the olive oil, parsley, celery, salt, and plenty of pepper. Serve at once.

il
FORNO

6 Sweets

dolci

LEFT: BAKERY *(FORNO)* IN VENTOTENE, THE SECOND PONTINE ISLAND

Tre sso' li bbôni bocconi:
fico, persica e mmeloni.

There are three good mouthfuls:
fig, peach, and melon.

—Roman saying

Any discussion of the last course on Latium's table must begin with the mention of fruit. First and foremost, the intensely flavored and often peppery dishes the natives love demand a chase with the ambrosial nectar of pears, peaches, apples, or whatever fruits are ripe and juicy in their harvest season. In Italy, however, fruits are not eaten with the hands. Rather, they are first placed on a small dish of their own, peeled, and cut with fork and knife into manageable pieces that can be eaten with delicacy and decorum. Grapes and cherries may be the only exceptions. From the time I was very small, I watched my Roman relatives peel their figs or perform precise surgeries to lift away the skins of their cactus pears (this requires some know-how). All of Italy has impeccable fruit manners, including Rome, whose citizens are sometimes considered by their countrymen to be somewhat coarse in their behavior, supposedly an inheritance from the unrefined populace of their ancestral city.

Besides fruit, there are sweets. There is a tendency toward more elaborate confections in the restaurants of Rome than in smaller cities and towns, because that city has always catered so much to tourists. In addition, the Romans themselves have a tendency to eat out rather than to cook elaborately at home, a habit that goes back to bygone days. In their ancient city, indoor ovens or stoves were prohibited because of the shoddy timber construction of the overcrowded tenement buildings, which burned down with alarming frequency. Even today, in a country where the bastion of good food is the home kitchen, Roman cooking in general, and baking in particular, is considered to be at its best in trattorias and pastry shops.

The *pasticcerìe* (pastry shops) and cafés of the towns and cities are more often than not where traditional cakes, biscotti, sweet buns, and various confections are to be found. Pastries are eaten not only as dessert, but also with the ritual afternoon cup of espresso or hot chocolate, or even for breakfast along with a cappuccino, tea, or hot chocolate.

No, no, I must live where there is no fire and the night is free from alarms!

—Juvenal; prominent Roman satirist, c. A.D. 125

Notwithstanding a reliance on professional baking for many sweets and confections, Rome and Latium hold on tightly to their baking traditions. Numerous desserts are associated with the Christian holiday calendar. *Mostaccioli* (honey-and-nut-based cookies) are eaten on Epiphany. *Frappe* (the fried sweet pasta dough of which every region has at least one version) are made for Carnival. Sweet breads are traditional at Christmas. Ricotta pies appear for Easter, and there are various fritters of sweetened rice or leavened dough for the many saint's days. The curious name of *mostaccioli* has nothing to do with mustaches, but with *mosto cotto*, the "cooked must" (unfermented juice) of the grape that is a by-product of wine making and an ingredient in many versions of the cookie.

A number of important specialties center around Latium's spectacular ricotta (page 20). These include ricotta pudding, ricotta pies, ricotta and spaghetti pudding, and ricotta gelato. Gelato, in which Rome excels in variety and sheer number of flavors (even surpassing the dazzling gelato displays of Florence), might be defined as ice cream, but it really isn't. Gelato is made with milk and eggs, while traditional ice cream contains cream. The quality of Roman gelato is not what it once was in this day and age when industrial methods are used to manufacture foods. Nevertheless, visitors to Rome would be shortchanging themselves if they didn't succumb to the beguiling *gelati* that are offered in astonishing spectrums of flavors and colors in every other bar. There are also the honest *granite*, fresh ices of fruit or coffee, that are so refreshing on sweltering summer afternoons.

It would be impossible to describe the countless *dolci* of Rome and its environs, and I have not tried to do so. Instead, I offer recipes that represent the spectrum of possibilities, from simple spoon desserts to the excellent *pizza dolce* of Easter, some sweet ricotta specialties, and biscotti.

Lemon Cream

crema limoncina

FOR 4 PEOPLE

3 extra-large eggs, separated

$1^3/_4$ cups, plus $^1/_2$ cup sifted confectioners' sugar

grated zest of 1 lemon

$^1/_3$ cup fresh lemon juice

pinch of salt

4 biscotti or wafers for serving

A simple and elegant spoon dessert, usually served with a biscotto *or wafer cookie slipped into each goblet.*

Place a medium stainless-steel bowl over a saucepan with 2 inches of simmering water. The water should not touch the bottom of the bowl. Add the egg yolks, the $1^3/_4$ cups sugar, the lemon zest, all but $^1/_8$ teaspoon of the lemon juice, and the salt. Using a whisk, beat the mixture into a fluffy cream, about 5 minutes. Remove from the heat and let cool. Cover with plastic wrap and refrigerate for 30 minutes.

In a large bowl and using clean beaters, combine the egg whites and reserved lemon juice. This will make the foam more stable. Beat until foamy, then beat in the remaining $^1/_2$ cup sugar a little at a time until it is all incorporated. Continue beating on high speed until stiff, glossy peaks form. Fold into the yolk mixture. Spoon the lemon cream into dessert goblets and refrigerate for 2 or 3 hours until ready to serve. Slip a *biscotto* into each, and serve.

Variation: Layer the cream in the goblets with fresh berries.

Ricotta Pudding

budino di ricotta

FOR 6 TO 8 PEOPLE

- 1/4 cup golden raisins
- 1/4 cup rum
- 1/2 cup fine plain biscotti or vanilla cookie crumbs for dusting pan
- 1 3/4 cups drained fresh whole-milk ricotta (see headnote)
- 4 extra-large eggs, separated
- 8 tablespoons sugar
- 1/3 cup all-purpose unbleached flour
- grated zest of 1 lemon
- 1/4 cup candied orange rind, cut into small dice
- pinch of salt
- 1 teaspoon cream of tartar
- ground cinnamon to taste

It follows that the exquisite sheep's milk ricotta Latium is famous for (page 20) would be put to many uses. With its dense, creamy texture, it is well suited to puddings and cheesecakes, of which I have provided a sampling in the two recipes that follow. The cow's milk ricotta available in our markets is thin in comparison, and should be placed in a sieve lined with a double layer of cheesecloth, covered with plastic wrap, and refrigerated to drain overnight before using for this recipe.

In a bowl, soak the raisins in the rum until they are nice and plump, about 40 minutes. Preheat the oven to 325° F. Generously butter an 8-inch springform pan. Add the cookie crumbs to the pan to coat it evenly, then tap out the excess.

In a large mixing bowl, beat the ricotta lightly. Gradually beat the egg yolks into the ricotta to blend thoroughly. Stir in 6 tablespoons of the sugar, the flour, lemon zest, candied orange rind, and soaked raisins and rum.

In a separate large bowl, beat the egg whites and salt until soft peaks form. Add the cream of tartar and remaining 2 tablespoons sugar and beat until stiff, glossy peaks form. Fold the egg whites into the ricotta mixture. Pour the ricotta mixture into the prepared pan, using a rubber spatula to spread the batter evenly. The batter should reach no more than halfway up the sides of the pan. Sprinkle with cinnamon.

Slide the pan onto the middle rack of the oven and bake until a toothpick inserted in the center of the cake comes out fairly clean and the top is golden, about 1 hour. Turn off the oven and leave the ricotta pudding inside with the door closed for 30 minutes. Remove from the oven and let cool completely. Remove the sides of the pan and slide the cake onto a serving plate. Cover with plastic wrap. Like *crostata di ricotta* (page 134), *budino di ricotta* needs to "age" before it is eaten in order for its flavor to develop. Refrigerate it for 2 days, then serve. It will keep, chilled, for up to 5 days.

Note: *Budino di ricotta* freezes well.

Sweet Ricotta Tart

crostata di ricotta

FOR 8 TO 10 PEOPLE

FOR THE PASTA FROLLA:

2 cups sifted pastry flour or unbleached all-purpose flour

1/2 cup sugar

pinch of salt

1/2 cup (1 stick) cold unsalted butter

1 large egg, beaten with 1 tablespoon milk

FOR THE FILLING:

2 1/2 cups drained fresh whole-milk ricotta

8 ounces mascarpone cheese at room temperature

3/4 cup, plus 2 tablespoons granulated sugar

1/3 cup all-purpose flour

4 extra-large eggs

1/4 cup rum

1/4 cup chopped bittersweet chocolate

1/4 cup chopped candied orange rind

1/2 teaspoon ground cinnamon

grated zest of 1 orange

grated zest of 1 lemon

1 cup heavy cream

confectioners' sugar for dusting

Crostata di ricotta *is a simple pie of northern Lazio, sometimes decorated with a lattice topcrust. The recipe was kindly provided by my aunt, Annette Messina. The crust is a classic* pasta frolla, *a sweet, cookie-like dough. As with most cheesecakes, this ricotta tart must be aged to develop its flavor. It should be made at least a day in advance, and is best eaten within 2 or 3 days of baking, but it will keep up to 1 week, chilled. In order to duplicate the texture of the ricotta of Lazio, the ricotta should be drained overnight (see headnote, page 133).*

To make the *pasta frolla:* Sift the flour, sugar, and salt together into a medium bowl. Using a pastry cutter or 2 dinner knives, cut in the butter until a crumblike mixture is formed. Using a fork, mix the egg mixture into the flour mixture until evenly moistened. Using your hands, gather about two-thirds of the dough into 1 ball and the remaining one-third into a second ball. Wrap each ball separately in plastic wrap and refrigerate for 1 hour or up to overnight before using.

Butter an 8-inch springform pan. Preheat the oven to 350° F.

Sprinkle a work surface lightly with flour and roll the larger ball of dough into a disk 1/8 inch thick. Place aluminum foil under the pan and crimp it around the sides of the pan to catch any leaks during baking. Fit the dough into the springform pan and crimp the edges. If making a lattice crust, roll out the second ball of dough into a disk 3/8 inch thick. Using a fluted pastry wheel, cut it into strips about 1/2 inch wide. Refrigerate the dough-lined pan and the strips of dough until ready for use.

To make the filling: In a large bowl, beat the ricotta and mascarpone together until well blended. Stir in the

continued

Sweet Ricotta Tart

continued

¾ cup granulated sugar and the flour. Beat in one egg at a time until each is fully incorporated into the mixture. Stir in the rum, chocolate, candied orange rind, cinnamon, and zests, and blend thoroughly.

In a deep bowl, beat the heavy cream with the 2 tablespoons granulated sugar until soft peaks are formed. Fold it into the ricotta mixture until blended. Pour the ricotta filling into the prepared pan and smooth the top evenly. Arrange the strips of dough in a diagonal lattice over the filling, trim where necessary, and pinch them onto the crust. Slide the pan onto the middle rack of the oven and bake until a skewer inserted into the center of the cake comes out clean, 1 hour to 1 hour and 15 minutes. Turn off the oven and leave the cake inside with the door closed for about 1 hour. Remove from the oven and let cool completely. Remove the sides of the springform pan. Slide the cake onto a cake platter. Cover with plastic wrap and refrigerate at least overnight before serving.

Before serving, dust the *crostata* with confectioners' sugar. The *crostata* is usually cut into small slices and accompanied with espresso.

Note: A Roman variation of *crostata di ricotta* is the beguilingly named *bocconotti* ("little mouthfuls") small tarts of *pasta frolla* crust filled with the mixture used for Ricotta Pudding (page 133).

Mostaccioli

mostaccioli

MAKES ABOUT 42 COOKIES

$2^1/_2$ cups all-purpose flour

$^3/_4$ cup sugar

$^1/_2$ teaspoon baking powder

$^1/_2$ teaspoon baking soda

pinch of salt

$^1/_2$ teaspoon freshly ground white or black pepper

$^3/_4$ cup ground walnuts

grated zest of 1 orange

$^1/_3$ cup honey

$^1/_4$ cup water

3 tablespoons extra-virgin olive oil

1 egg, beaten

Mostaccioli *can take many forms, from chocolate biscuits to miniature layer cakes separated with rice paper, but common to all is honey as a sweetener. An ancient tradition throughout Italy and Lazio as well, they are typically simple, firm cookies designed for dunking in sweet wine. This version, spiced with pepper, is based on the* mostaccioli *made in Giuliana Quattrocchi's bakery, Dal Borgo, in Farfa.*

To make the dough, combine the flour, sugar, baking powder, baking soda, salt, pepper, walnuts, and orange zest in a mixing bowl. Mix together the honey, water, olive oil, and egg in a small bowl. Add the honey mixture to the dry ingredients and continue mixing until the dough begins to hold together. Do not mix excessively or the *mostaccioli* will become tough. The dough will be somewhat sticky. Turn it out onto a floured work surface and knead lightly until smooth. Form the dough into a ball, cover with plastic wrap, and leave it to rest at room temperature for about 30 minutes.

Preheat the oven to 350° F. Line two baking sheets with parchment paper.

Lightly flour the work surface once again and, with your hands, form the dough into a log, about 2 inches thick and 12 inches long. Press on the roll of dough lightly and use a sharp knife to cut it into horizontal slices, each about ¼-inch thick. You will have to cut only two or three at a time to prevent the cookies from sticking together. Transfer the cookies to the lined baking sheets as soon as they are cut. Bake them in the middle of the oven for about 15 minutes, or until they are lightly colored. Lift the paper off the pans and cool the *mostaccioli* on racks.

Permit the *mostaccioli* to cool for 1 hour, then store them in a tin separated between layers of wax paper.

Sweet Easter Pizza

pizza di Pasqua

MAKES 2 LOAVES

FOR THE SPONGE:

$^1/_2$ cup warm milk (105° to 115° F) or lukewarm milk (80° to 90° F)

$1^1/_2$ packages ($3^1/_2$ teaspoons) active dry yeast, or $1^1/_2$ cakes compressed yeast

$^1/_2$ cup bread flour

FOR THE DOUGH:

sponge, above

10 extra-large egg yolks

scant $^2/_3$ cup sugar

$^1/_2$ cup (1 stick) plus 1 tablespoon unsalted butter at room temperature

$^1/_2$ cup milk

grated zest of 4 lemons

2 teaspoons pure vanilla extract

2 tablespoons rose water

2 teaspoons ground cinnamon (optional)

$3^1/_3$ cups bread flour

1 extra-large egg white, lightly beaten

This delicious, delicate sweet bread bears no resemblance to savory pizza. Rather, it resembles panettone, *but is less buttery. Once, lard was used in place of butter, and in many parts of Latium, it still is. The original recipe calls for* rosòlio, *literally "rose oil," an alcoholic liqueur based on rose petals and honey that dates back to the fifteenth century.* Rosòlio *is lovely in sweet breads, cakes, and confections, but it is not exported. I like to use rose water in its place, although it is a pale substitute for the real thing. One of the endless variations of this bread relies on cinnamon for flavoring, which may be included here if you like.* Pizza di Pasqua *is traditionally eaten on Easter morning with boiled eggs, which symbolize rebirth, along with slices of salami. The recipe should be started early in the day, as some 5 or 6 hours are necessary for the rise alone. It is better to use a heavy-duty electric mixer than to work by hand, as the dough requires extensive kneading before the first rise.*

To make the sponge: In the bowl of an electric mixer, stir the warm milk and yeast together until the yeast is dissolved. Let stand until foamy, about 12 minutes. Stir in the flour. Cover tightly with plastic wrap and let stand until the mixture has doubled in bulk and looks very spongy in texture, about 1 hour.

To make the dough: Fit the mixer with the paddle attachment. With the machine running, add the egg yolks to the sponge, one at a time. Add the sugar and beat until creamy, then gradually add in the butter, milk, lemon zest, vanilla, rose water, cinnamon (if using), and flour. Beat on medium speed for at least 12 minutes, stopping occasionally to scrape down the sides of the bowl. After beating, the dough should barely stick to your hands, as the large quantity of egg yolks will make it very elastic.

Cover the bowl tightly with plastic wrap, then place a clean kitchen towel over it. Let rise in a warm, draft-free place until tripled in bulk, about 3 hours.

Generously butter 2 loaf pans. Punch the dough down and turn it out onto a floured work surface. Grease your hands with butter or olive oil and knead the dough to work out the large bubbles, about 5 minutes. It should remain very soft, almost sticky, and elastic. Divide the dough in half and place each half in one of the buttered loaf pans. Cover the pans tightly with plastic wrap and cover with the kitchen towels. Let rise once again until the dough doubles in bulk, about 2½ hours.

Preheat the oven to 375° F. Brush the surface of each loaf with the egg white and slide the pans onto the middle rack of the oven. Bake until golden, about 12 minutes. Cover loosely with aluminum foil and bake about 20 minutes longer, until the tops of the loaves balloon into a great dome and are golden brown. Remove from the oven and let cool for about 5 minutes, then remove carefully from the pans. Place on wire racks to cool.

Cristo è risuscitato, allegramente!
In sta giornata nun s'abbadi a spesa
E nun se pensi a guai un accidente
Brodetto, ova, salame, zuppa ingresa,
Carciofi, granelli e' rimanente
Tutto a la grolia della Santa Chiesa.

Christ has risen, merrily!
On this day, let's not fret about expenses,
Let's forget our trouble a while.
Soup, eggs, salami and trifle,
Artichokes, grains and everything else
All for the glory of the Holy Church.

—Gioacchino Belli, Roman poet

Dal Borgo's Little Walnut Cakes

pastarelle con noci Dal Borgo

MAKES 2 1/2 DOZEN COOKIES

1/2 cup (1 stick) plus 2 tablespoons unsalted butter, cut into small pieces

3 1/4 cups all-purpose flour

scant 1 cup sugar

1 teaspoon baking powder

1/4 teaspoon salt

3 extra-large eggs

1 teaspoon vanilla extract

12 ounces finely chopped walnuts

The enchanting town of Farfa in Rieti Province rises from the slopes of Mount Buzio in the Sabine and has a sweeping view of the Tiber Valley. Besides its particularly ancient history—it was the seat of King Tito Tazio, who reigned during the years of the war between the Sabines and the Romans, circa 760 B.C.—it is noteworthy for a number of things. One is its splendid abbey, the Abbazia di Farfa, which was originally constructed in 420 B.C. as a pagan temple. According to local legend, a dragon used to fly over its ruins until the place was consecrated as a Christian abbey. Also of note in Farfa is a remarkable olive tree that is over 2,000 years old. It is 22 feet in circumference, 33 feet high, and produces nearly 3 tons of olives yearly. Another jewel in Farfa's crown is Giuliana Quatrocchi's bakery, Dal Borgo, which makes some of the best confections around.

NOTE: *While the dough for these cookies can be made by hand, it is far easier to use a heavy-duty electric mixer.*

In a large bowl, combine the butter, flour, sugar, baking powder, and salt. Use a pastry cutter or 2 dinner knives to cut in the butter until the mixture is fine and crumbly. In a small bowl, beat 2 of the eggs and the vanilla together and stir into the dry ingredients. Mix the dough just until all the ingredients come together. Turn the mixture out onto a floured work surface and knead for a minute or two by hand to form a cohesive dough. It should be somewhat sticky. Wrap the dough in plastic wrap and refrigerate for 1 hour.

Preheat the oven to 350° F. Line 2 baking sheets with parchment paper. Spread the walnuts out on a piece of waxed paper.

Dust your hands with flour and shape the dough into 3 ropes, each about 1 1/2 inches in diameter. Cut each into 2-inch pieces. In a small bowl, beat the remaining egg. Dip each of the pieces into the beaten egg, then roll in the walnuts to coat evenly. Place the cookies about 1 1/2 inches apart on the prepared baking sheet.

Bake the cookies until they are lightly colored, 12 to 15 minutes. Slip the parchment, with the cookies, off each baking sheet and let cool on wire racks. Let stand for 2 minutes before peeling the cookies off.

Variation: Dust the cookies with confectioners' sugar before serving.

RNA DEL CAMPO

soste

Eating and Sleeping Places

Eating and Sleeping Places in Rome and Latium

EATING IN ROME AND LATIUM

If anything has endured from the food habits of the ancient Romans until this day, it is the *osteria* tradition. This type of informal neighborhood eatery was an outgrowth of the housing problems of the populace. Public housing, called *insulae,* was a shaky affair. The cheap, multistory tenements constructed of timber and mud bricks lacked plumbing, insulation, and indoor exhaust or flue systems. The poor engineering and conditions of overcrowding made the *insulae* vulnerable to fire, and the buildings collapsed or burned down frequently. Cooking indoors was prohibited, so a tradition arose of eating and drinking meals in informal eateries and taverns at appointed times and buying carryout food to eat at home (the Romans invented "takeout" and the "doggie bag"). Breakfast (usually water, perhaps with bread), and lunch, *prandium,* were light affairs. There was one large meal, *cena,* "dinner," taken before sunset. In any case, the Romans spent most of the day outside and made social events of the day's ritual activities (including the toilet and the bath).

Besides the need to eat out and the legendary penchant for the table, there are other historic causes for the large number of eating establishments that proliferated in the city and along the well-traveled routes to Rome. The metropolis was the center of the world and drew streams of visitors on matters of government, commerce, and religion. The city became a world center of hospitality. In addition, since 1870, Rome has also been the seat of national government, which has brought about a plethora of restaurants specializing in regional cuisines from all over Italy.

ROME, CAMPO DE' FIORI, TABLES OUTSIDE WINE BAR, PIAZZA AND PALAZZO FARNESE IN THE BACKGROUND

The sheer volume of tourists who cross the thresholds of Roman eating establishments today discourages what has come to be called "slow food": authentic local cuisine. Once, the very definition of a *trattoria* was that it had a neighborhood character. But with the decline of home cooking and the proliferation of fast foods, restaurant food has become increasingly commercial. The good Roman restaurants are known mostly to "real" Romans, as they are wont to call themselves. Nevertheless, I offer recommendations for some establishments that have consistently maintained high standards. Outside the city, there are many excellent restaurants that are only too happy for business, and where good provincial cooking can be found.

Throughout Italy, but especially in Rome, the traveler may be confused by the many types of restaurants that exist. Here are the differences, in a nutshell. The *bar* bears no similarity to any Anglo establishment with the same title, except that food and drink are taken either standing up at the counter, or sitting down at casual tables. This is where one goes for gelato, coffee, a simple pastry, sandwiches of various types, sundry snacks, and freshly squeezed orange or grapefruit juice *(spremuta d'arancia, di pompelmo,* respectively), a tradition that is slowly being replaced by the sale of bottled fruit juices. Some *bars* offer hot snacks, too. Originally, the *osteria* (also *hostaria)* was a place for drinking wine, but today it can offer food as well, even if the menu is somewhat streamlined. Then there is the *trattoria,* originally an informal mom-and-pop establishment where *nonna* made gnocchi on a table at the back of the kitchen. The *ristorante* (restaurant) is generally, although not necessarily, formal. Formal *ristoranti* can be pricey, but Italian casual attire is acceptable (American casual attire, such as running shoes and T-shirts, are not). The *rosticceria* sells take-out food. Some *rosticcerie* and *bars* have a *tavola calda* ("hot table"), where people can eat delicious prepared foods "on the go."

CAMPO DE' FIORI AREA

Ar Galletto, Piazza Farnese 102. Tel: 06.686.1714. Traditional Roman cooking *(trippa pajata, carciofi),* relaxed ambience, outdoor tables in good weather, right across from the Palazzo Farnese, with no cars or traffic allowed on the piazza: a rarity in Rome.

Da Pierluigi, Piazza de'Ricci 144. Tel: 06.686.1302. Located on one of the quaintest piazzas in Rome. Traditional dishes, including *pasta e fagioli, minestra con l'arzilla, soppressa di polpo, filetto al limone, torta di cioccolato con panna.*

Il Cardinale, via delle Carceri 6. Tel: 06.687.8430. Closed Sundays and holidays. Specializes in cooking vegetables from the Campo de'Fiori market, and in Jewish specialties (the Jewish ghetto is not far away).

Costanza, piazza del Paradiso 65. Tel: 06.6880.1002. Closed Sundays and in August. At the entrance of the Theater of Pompeo, where Julius Caesar was murdered, this restaurant serves excellent Roman cooking.

La Carbonara, piazza Campo de'Fiori 23. Tel: 06.686.4783. Closed Tuesdays and in August. A rustic *trattoria* that cooks fresh vegetables from the Campo de'Fiori market, as well as Roman specialties.

Ristorante Camponeschi, piazza Farnese 50. Tel: 06.687.4927. Closed Sundays and in August. Web site: www.ristorantecamponeschi.it. One of the most elegant restaurants in Rome, serving Roman cooking and international cuisine; specializing in fish. Reservations a must.

Vecchia Roma, piazza Campitelli 18. Tel: 06.686.4604. Closed Wednesdays and the last two weeks in August. A quintessentially Roman restaurant serving classic Roman food.

COLISEUM AREA

Al Gladiatore, via del Santi Quattro 48. Tel: 06.7720.9496. Rustic, busy *osteria* serving popular Roman food.

JEWISH GHETTO AREA

Al Pompiere, via Santa Maria de'Calderari 38. Tel: 06.686.8377. Closed Sundays and in August. The restaurant, on the second floor of a seventeenth-century palazzo in the heart of the Roman ghetto, serves Roman cooking and a few Jewish specialties. The menu includes *bucatini all'amatriciana, carbonara, carciofi alla giudia, frittura.*

Evangelista, via delle Zoccolette 11. Tel: 06.687.5810. A celebrity stop famous for Jewish specialties and Roman cooking.

Piperno, Monte de' Cenci 9. Tel: 06.6880.6629. Closed Sunday evenings, Christmas, Easter, and in August. The most famous, and most expensive, restaurant in the ghetto, serving Jewish and Roman specialties.

PANTHEON AREA

Le Volte, piazza Rondini 47. Tel: 06.687.7408. Closed Tuesdays. Specializes in Roman pizzas and simple Roman cooking.

Fortunato as Pantheon, around the corner from the Pantheon. Tel: 06.679.2788. Closed Sundays and holidays. Serves Roman specialties.

SPANISH STEPS AREA

Otello alla Concordia, via della Croce 8. Tel: 06.679.1178. Closed Sundays. Alfresco dining on a covered terrace. *Antipasti* are a specialty of the house.

Nino, via Borgognona 11. Tel: 06.679.5676. Closed Sundays and in August. This casual, busy place at the foot of the Spanish Steps is a favorite of my colleague, inveterate food critic and travel writer Fred Ferretti, for its straightforward, succulent fare. Granted, it's a Tuscan restaurant in the middle of Rome, but Nino makes an unbeatable *penne all'arrabbiata*. Popular dishes here are a terrific baked vegetable terrine and a superb *salame Toscano*. You need to go early because Nino is always crowded at the height of the lunch and dinner hours. There are so many lackluster restaurants in this busy tourist district that it's good to keep Nino in mind when you find yourself in the area.

TRASTEVERE VICINITY

Ristorante Paris, piazza San Calisto 7. Tel: 06.581.5378. Located south of Trastevere, serving typical Roman food and Roman-Jewish dishes, including fabulous *fritture* (the chef once cooked in the famous Piperno restaurant in the Jewish ghetto).

Sora Lella, via Ponte di Quattro Capi 16. Tel: 06.686.1601. Closed Saturdays and in August. On the Isola Tiberna between the Jewish ghetto and Trastevere stands Sora Lella, a long-established family-run restaurant with a devoted following of locals and return travelers alike. Casual setting. Excellent, sophisticated treatment of classic Roman fare and original dishes.

VATICAN AREA

Da Marcello, via dei Campani 12. Tel: 06.446.3311. Closed Saturday nights, Sundays, and in August. One of the better *osterie* in the area serving traditional Roman food.

NEAR THE TREVI FOUNTAIN

Moro, vicolo delle Bollette 13. Tel: 06.678.3495. Closed Sundays, holidays, and in August. This famous little place opened in 1929 despite the great economic crisis of the times, and its doors have been open ever since. It is as rustic now as then, serving robust and marvelous local dishes while the old white-haired man who owns the place plays cards at a table and proprietarily surveys the scene. Come with cash. The absence of modern conveniences has kept the food terrifically honest, but in the same spirit, credit cards are not accepted.

Sleeping in Rome and Latium

Hotels in Rome, as in other large cities filled with tourists, can be very expensive, and are often not within walking distance of the main sights. Travel agents that specialize in travel to Italy are well worth seeking out for booking services as well as for their expertise in providing information about the locales of specific hotels and accommodations.

This is not by any means a comprehensive directory of accommodations in Rome and Latium. It is a personal list of fine and centrally located hotels that also have some historical character, extrapolated from my visits to the region over the years. In addition, I have given some suggestions for rural accommodations in Latium that evoke the history and flavor of their surroundings. Reservations are always advisable.

TRAVEL SERVICES

Magna Travel Services, 60–56 Fresh Pond Road, Maspeth, New York 11378. Tel: 718.381.4500; fax: 718.504.6056; e-mail: info@gomagna.com. Specialists in travel to Italy.

HOTELS IN ROME

Bettoja Hotels, owned and run by cookbook writer and cooking teacher Jo Bettoja and her husband, are all located in central Rome. This is a family business (the largest family-owned hotel group in Italy) that is run with care and attention to good food. The five Bettoja hotels are all within walking distance of the Colosseum, Opera House, the via Veneto, Spanish Steps, and subways, bus, railroad, and airline terminals. A list of the five hotels, their locations, and booking information follow. New York Office: MPR, 130 E. Ninety-fourth St., Suite 3A, New York, New York 10128. Tel: 212.860.5445, 800.783.6904. Fax: 212.860.4544. e-mail hb@bettojahotels.it.

Hotel Mediterraneo, via Cavour 15. Four stars, "superior." On the Esquilino Hill, the highest of the seven hills of Rome.

Massimo D'Azeglio, via Cavour 18. Four stars. Late nineteenth-century architecture and design, housing an important collection of prints and paintings from the Italian Risorgimento era. The hotel restaurant is considered one of the best in the city, and has an extensive wine cellar.

Atlantico Hotel, via Cavour 23. Four stars. Bar and restaurant on the premises.

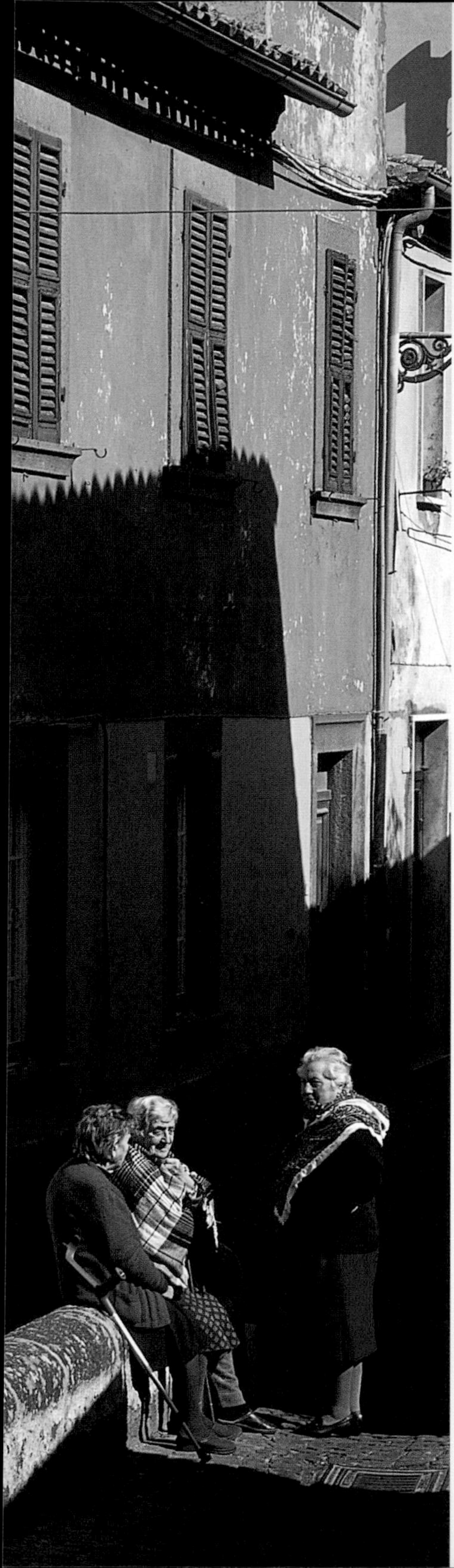

San Giorgio Hotel, via G. Amendola 61. Four stars. Rooms with terraces, and accommodations well suited to business travel.

Nord Nuova Roma Hotel, via G. Amendola 3. Three stars. Faces the Roman Archeological Museum and across the piazza from the Museum of the Baths of Diocletian and the Opera House.

The Hotel Raphael, Largo Febo 2, near the piazza Navona. Tel: 06.541.233. An established and charming old-fashioned hotel that has always drawn a discriminating clientele.

The Hotel Columbus, via della Conciliazione 33. Tel: 06.686.5435; fax 06.686.4874. This sumptuous fifteenth-century palazzo, formerly the residence of Pope Julius II, is a block away from St. Peter's Basilica and still a favorite of visiting clergy. Although it is filled with splendid appointments (the dining area has its original frescoes), the bedrooms are simple, which accounts for their relatively modest cost.

The Santa Chiara, via Santa Chiara 21. Tel: 06.687.2979; fax: 06.687.3144. An elegant old hotel near the Pantheon, and within walking distance of many of Rome's famous sites, The Santa Chiara offers large and small rooms, necessary modern conveniences, and three apartments with kitchens and terraces.

Hotel del Sole al Pantheon, piazza della Rotonda 63. Tel: 06.678.0441; fax: 06.69.94.0689. Also in the neighborhood of the Pantheon, this tasteful old hotel has drawn a selective clientele of literati over the years who appreciate its ancient tradition and subdued charm. The rooms are bright and pleasant, with modern comforts, and the rates are relatively reasonable.

Hassler-Villa Medici, piazza Trinità dei Monti 6. Tel: 06.699.340. Located at the top of the Spanish Steps, the Hassler-Villa Medici, the most sumptuous and expensive hotel in Rome, has hosted American presidents, international dignitaries, film stars, and royalty. It has one of the best restaurants in Rome.

Hotel Portoghesi, via dei Portoghesi 1. Tel: 06.686.4231; fax: 06.687.6976; e-mail: portoghesi@venere.it. Named after the adjacent church, Chiesa Nazionale Portoghese, the hotel is housed in a late-sixteenth-century palazzo behind the piazza Navona in an atmospheric neighborhood of seventeenth-century houses and narrow cobblestone streets. The rooms are pleasant, some with period antiques. The dining room has a terrace, where, in good weather, meals are served alfresco.

BED-AND-BREAKFASTS IN ROME AND LATIUM

Bed-and-breakfast establishments have long been an alternative to high-priced hotels in Britain, Ireland, Germany, and Austria. This style of hostelry is a recent but growing development in Italy. It is a lovely way to get off the tourist route, and it can place a traveler in a town or in the countryside in private accommodations in actual homes. Bed-and-breakfast traveling can be unreliable without a guide, but there are numerous agencies and Web sites (in Italian and English) with color photographs of accommodations in every category from farmhouses to castles and rooms to private apartments with kitchens.

Bed and Breakfast La Chiesuola (literally the "itty-bitty church"), strada Chiesuola 16, Bagnaia (VT). Tel: 0761.28.95.24; e-mail: lachiesuola@libero.it. Eleonora Paolucci and Corrado Leporatti's bed-and-breakfast is less than an hour's drive north of Rome in the hilly heart of Etruria, 1,970 feet above sea level, behind an estate where Capuchin monks once paused in their wanderings for shelter and spiritual nourishment. Eleonora grows her own organic vegetables and cooks superb local dishes. She also makes her own *salumi* and liqueurs along with cakes and breakfast pastries that would put the best bakery in town to shame. If you can tear yourself away from Eleonora's cooking, Corrado will take you on walking tours along the paths of the stupendous surrounding Cimini Mountains, or to the famous castles and villas of Tuscia, the Papal Palace in Viterbo, and the most famous Etruscan necropoli and museums of Tarquinia and Viterbo. Organized outings include visits to the nearby therapeutic thermal baths; hunting for antiques, chestnuts, or mushrooms; and splendid rides through the countryside on horseback. Bomarzo, a magical park full of giant grotesque statues; Villa Lante, the Renaissance palace famous for its gardens and fountains; and many surrounding medieval villages are close by.

FACING PAGE:
MONTEFIASCONE, A HILL TOWN NORTH OF ROME, WOMEN CHATTING IN VIA PIANA

Elegant Etruria at www.elegantetruria.com is another source of bed-and-breakfast accommodations. Hosted by Mary Jane Cryan, a travel writer and resident of Viterbo, the site offers listings and booking services for lodgings in historic village apartments, student hostels, country villas and castles, charming small hotels, and farmhouse holiday apartments for family groups.

AGRITURISM IN LAZIO

Farm holidays are a fast-growing cottage industry in Italy. A source for agriturismo accommodations in Latium is Lazio (English edition), a guidebook published by the Touring Club of Italy. Touring Club Italiano, corso Italia 10, 20122 Milan, Italy. Web site: www.touring club.it.

Agiturismo La Riserva Montebello, strada Orvietana, Km. 3, 01023 Bolsena (VT). Tel: 0761.79.89.65; fax: 0761.79.94.92. Book through Magna Travel: tel: 718.381.4500; e-mail: info@gomagna.com. This is a lovely restored farmhouse-hotel situated on seventy-five acres of woodland, olive groves, kiwifruit orchards, and gardens on the slopes of the hills overlooking Bolsena, 900 feet above sea level. The focus of the *pensione's* menu is freshwater fish, which is plucked from the lake only hours before it is cooked. The food here is simple, tasty, and delicious, based on the excellent olive oil and other products of the farm. There are three swimming pools, sailing, horseback riding, and other activities on site. The Etruscan city of Tarquinia with its awesome ruins and museum; the Farnese Palace; and the tiny enchanting papal island Isola Bisentia are a short drive away.

sagre

Festivals

Food is an important feature of all Italian festivals, but many public events are organized for the sole purpose of celebrating particular important local products, along with traditional dishes and the local wine. Entire towns may turn out to cook and feast on porcini, chestnuts, or prosciutto, to taste and drink wine; to usher in the harvest, or to greet the winter sleep. Then there are the processions and festivals organized on a grand scale to celebrate a patron saint. The harvest *sagre* are particularly appealing, as the streets are filled with beautiful aromas and volunteers are busy dishing up plates of food. The *prezzo fisso*, "fixed price," is always a bargain even if the food gets tired by the end of the night. Besides the festivals I have highlighted, there are hundreds of others that take place in the towns and villages of Latium throughout the year.

JANUARY

Tuscania (Viterbo): Fritter festival *(sagra delle frittelle)*. A hill town that has been inhabited continuously since the Etruscan period, Tuscania has 7,622 inhabitants who are deeply proud of their ancient roots.

FEBRUARY

Castel di Tora (Rieti): Polenta festival *(sagra del polentone)*.

MARCH

Cineto R. (Rome): A polenta festival *(sagra della polenta)* takes place in this town, which was founded by the ancient Equi people and was conquered by Rome in A.D. 332.

Montecompatri (Rome): On March 19 every year, ancient taverns *(osterie)*, which are called *frasche* in this area, are reconstructed to celebrate the local wines (Montecompatri Colonna) and artisanal foods *(le fraschette)*.

APRIL

Ladispoli (Rome): An artichoke festival *(sagra del carciofo romanesco)* is held for three days in the second half of April. The precise date is linked to the maturation time of the artichokes that grow between Ladispoli and Cervèteri. The celebration has an international flavor, and the artichokes are cooked in a different way on every street corner in town. Folk dancing and fireworks are part of the festivities.

Tarquinia (Viterbo): In the second half of April, *La Merca*, a cowboys' tournament, takes place in the locality of Roccaccia. The spectacle, which has taken place every year since medieval times, is arranged by Italian *butteri*, "cowboys," who tend the wild cattle and bulls in the nearby Lazio Maremma. (Also in this area, for ten days in mid-August, there are competitions of riding, roping, and branding.) Tolfa stands on one of the undulating hills in the Tolfa Mountains, a group of peaks in the Sabatini Mountain range.

MAY

Barbarano Romano (Viterbo): On the first Sunday of May is the *festa dell'attozzata*, held in front of the church of San Giuliano. The local shepherds cook *attozata*, a soup of ricotta made from their sheep's milk. Handmade local salami, sausages, and pancetta *"alla contadina,"* in the style of the local farmers, are also featured.

Gerano (Rome): This is one of the towns that holds an *infiorata*, a display of flower "paintings" on the street. The event takes place every year on the first Sunday after the Feast of Saint Mark, April 25.

Nepi (Viterbo): A pecorino festival *(sagra del pecorino)* and salami festival *(sagra del salame cotto)*.

JUNE

Genzano di Roma: In this Castelli Romani town, a festival of flower art-work on the streets *(infiorata)* is held on one of the days of Corpus Domini. The stupendous "paintings," made with different colors of flower petals, line the via Italo Berardi, which leads to the church of Santa Maria della Cima.

Nemi (Rome): A strawberry festival *(sagra delle fragole)* is held on the first Sunday of June. The entire city is filled with the perfume of straw-berries, as country girls in traditional costume hand them out on the streets. The *sagra* is followed by an exquisite flower show, *tarantella* folk dancing, and acrobats in the streets of nearby Fontana delle Coste.

JULY

Ariccia (Rome): On the last weekend in July, the *Sagra delle Cannacce* is held. *Cannacce* are thick handmade noodles particular to the town. A grand finale to the *sagra* takes place the next day with a Sunday market in the main piazza, and in the evening, a musical spectacle.

Bolsena (Viterbo): For three days in mid-July, there is a fish festival on the lakefront. Stands are set up to sell various local freshwater fish specialties, including *sbroscia* (fish soup), and fried fish.

Minturno (Latina): *Regne* are handfuls of grains tossed into the earth for sowing wheat, thus *sagra delle regne* celebrates the wheat harvest. The festivities, held on the second Sunday in July, are in honor of the Madonna delle Grazie, the patron saint of the town. After a series of rituals symbolizing gratitude to the Madonna, there is a dinner of local artisanal sausages and *salame*, and bread that has been blessed by the priest in honor of the wheat harvest.

AUGUST

Amatrice (Rieti): The famous dish *spaghetti all'amatriciana* was born in this town, which was once a major Roman center. A festival *(sagra degli spaghetti)* is held on the last Saturday in August, during which the most celebrated masters of *spaghetti all'amatriciana* cook the dish in the main piazza and distribute it free to all who attend.

Cervèteri (Rome): This famous Etruscan town, which juts out of the tufa rock on the slopes of the Tolfa Mountains, holds a grape festival *(sagra dell'uva)* on the last Sunday of August.

Fara in Sabina: A roast pork festival *(sagra della porchetta)*; also, an olive festival on the last Sunday of August.

Civitavecchia (Rome): A fish festival *(sagra del mare)* takes place along the street facing the sea. Fish are cooked in a huge skillet and given out to everyone who passes by.

Montefiascone (Viterbo): A wine festival *(sagra del vino)* is held from August 1 to 15 for the celebrated wine made here, Est! Est! Est!

Onano (Viterbo): A lentil festival *(sagra della lenticchia)* is held here in celebration of the local crop during the week of August 15 *(Ferragosto)*, the national summer holiday.

Poggio Catino (Rieti): The *sagra della panzanella* (bread salad festival) coincides with the feast of the patron saint Maria Santissima Assunta, August 14 to 17.

Segni (Rome): A *porchetta* festival *(sagra della porchetta)* is held on August 9. Roasted pork is cooked in the central piazza while handicrafts are sold along the streets, all to the sound of folk music in the open air.

SEPTEMBER

Cerreto Laziale (Rome): A *pizzarelle* festival *(sagra delle pizzarelle)* is held the second Sunday in September, coinciding with a religious celebration, *festa della Madonna delle Grazie. Pizzarelle* are not small pizzas, but homemade pasta made with three parts white flour to one part corn-meal. The dough is rolled out thinly and cut into long ribbons. After cooking it is sauced with *pistacchia*, a tomato sauce made with a pesto of garlic, olive oil, and red pepper, or various tomato sauces using lamb, snails, or *baccalà*.

Lanuvio (Rome): On the last Sunday of the month, a festival of the grape and wine is held to celebrate the local wine, Colli Lanuvini *(sagra dell' uva e del vino)*.

OCTOBER

Capena (Rome): On the first Sunday of every October, the town celebrates the grape harvest with a procession of allegorical carts, grape pickers, and bagpipe players. There is also wine tasting and food.

Marino: A grape festival *(sagra dell'uva)*, held on the first Sunday of October. The celebration of the grape and of wine is carried on in a carnival-like atmosphere. On this day, the town fountain spouts wine instead of water.

Olevano Romano (Rome): On the first Sunday of October, a grape festival is held in honor of the Madonna of the Rosary *(sagra dell'uva)*

Posta Fibreno (Frosinone): A grape festival takes place here on the first Sunday of October *(sagra dell'uva)*.

Zagarolo (Rome): This town, known for its sweet red wine, among others, holds a wine tasting and festival. The fountains spout wine, and there are reenactments of peasant life and conferences on agriculture. This spectacular festival *(sagra dell'uva e mostra dei vini tipici locali)* takes place on the first weekend in October.

Lo vedi?
Ecco Marino,
la sagra c'é dell'uva,
fontane che danno vino,
quant'abbondanza c'é.

Do you see it?
Here is Marino,
the festival of grapes,
fountains spout wine,
what abundance!

—A song of the Castelli Romani, as quoted in *'Na gita a li Castelli (A Tour of the Castelli)*

NOVEMBER

Nerola (Rome): An olive oil festival *(sagra dell'olio d'oliva)*.

DECEMBER

Bomarzo (Viterbo): The *Sagra del tozzetto* is held one week before Christmas. *Tozzetti* are hazelnut or almond biscotti made all over central Italy, but every family seems to have its own recipe for it.

Canino (Viterbo): The olive oil festival *(sagra dell'olivo)*, featuring the local olive oil, is held during the second week of December.

Gaeta (Latina): *Lo sciuscio*, a musical and folkloric festival, takes place during Christmas week. Ancient musical instruments are played by the musicians.

Frascati (Rome): On the second and third day of the last week in December, the town holds a public wine tasting of the local *vino novello*, new wine.

Ponzano R. (Rome): The bruschetta festival *(sagra della bruschetta)* is held on December 7 and 8, on the heels of the festival for the patron saint.

Cooking Schools and Wine Courses

IN THE UNITED STATES

La Vera Cucina, Julia della Croce's Italian Cooking School, Rockland County, New York, and New York City. Tel: 845.634.3172; e-mail: julia@juliadellacroce.com. Web site: www.juliadellacroce.com. Classes in Italian regional cooking. Instruction by award-winning cooking teacher Julia della Croce, and celebrated guest teachers of regional Italian cooking. Classes in wine appreciation. Referral service for professional Italian chefs, Italian food consultants, Italian food and travel photographers, and Italian food, wine, and olive oil experts.

Anna Teresa Callen Italian Cooking School, 59 West 12th Street, New York, New York 10011. Tel: 212.929.5640. Anna Teresa Callen is a native Italian who has authored numerous books about Italian cooking. She is an authority on regional Italian cooking, and a charismatic and engaging cooking teacher.

The Magazine of La Cucina Italiana Cooking School, 230 Fifth Avenue, New York, New York 10001. Tel: 212.725.8764, toll-free: 888.742.2373; e-mail: piacere@earthlink.net. Demonstration classes with well-known Italian chefs and cookbook authors. Classes in wine and olive oil appreciation.

IN ITALY

Casa Caponetti, tenuta del Guado Antico, Tuscània (VT). Tel: 076.143.4792; fax: 076.1442.44247; e-mail: caponetti@caponetti.com. Always open. Fluent English spoken. Country accommodations and cooking classes on the Caponetti estate in the Etruscan valley of Tuscia, which D. H. Lawrence called "the most beautiful view in all of Italy." Cooking classes taught by Laura Caponetti, who holds an advanced degree in Italian gastronomy and has been a restaurant and hotel consultant. Equestrian instruction offered by the master of the house, one of Italy's best known horse trainers and riding instructors.

Cook Italy, Fontana del Papa, 00059 Tolfa (RM) Lazio. Tel/fax: 076.693.455; e-mail: info@fontanadelpapa.it. Web site: www.cookitaly.it. Book through Elegant Etruria (see page 150). Bed-and-breakfast accommodations and cooking classes in a restored historic house on Assuntina Antonacci's estate in the Viterbo countryside. The cooks are Italian women of the area. Assuntina's husband is an architect who conducts tours of the area, and her daughter, a certified rock climber, takes groups for hikes and climbing expeditions in the area.

La Toretta, via Mazzini 7, Casperia (RI) Lazio. Book through Elegant Etruria (see below). La Toretta, located in the quaint, car-free village of Casperia, can be reached directly by train from Rome's airport. Art historian Maureen Scheda holds hands-on cooking classes in the kitchen of her beautiful historic home, which has been transformed into an elegant bed-and-breakfast.

Elegant Etruria. Web site: www.elegantetruria.com. Travel writer Mary Jane Cryan organizes personalized day trips out of Rome for small tourist and business groups. Programs can include concerts, lunches, spas, wine tastings, and visits to artisans and olive oil mills. Provides information on Etruscan treks, painting and ceramics courses, and insiders' tours of Rome and Etruria.

To Italy with Julia. Tel: 845.634.3172; e-mail: julia@juliadellacroce.com; Web site: www.juliadellacroce.com. Unique culinary and cultural tours of Italy with Julia della Croce, award-winning author-teacher.

Mail-Order Sources

Sources for Italian Cooking Equipment, Ingredients, and Products

Bridge Kitchenware
214 East 52nd Street
New York, New York 10022
Tel: 212.688.4220
Fax: 212.758.5387
Web site: www.bridgekitchenware.com
A New York City culinary landmark that sells cookware for professional and home cooks.

Buon Italia
Chelsea Market, 75 Ninth Avenue
New York, New York 10011
Tel: 212.633.9090
Fax: 212.633.9717
Web site: www.buonitalia.com
High-end regional Italian food specialties and hard-to-find Italian food imports. Mail order, Internet, retail, and restaurant trade sales. Orders shipped.

Coluccio & Sons
1220 60th Street
Brooklyn, New York 11219
Tel: 718.436.6700
Italian food specialties. Product list available.

D'Artagnan
280 Wilson Avenue
Newark, New Jersey 07105
Tel: 800.327.8246
Fax: 973.465.1870
E-mail: email@dartagnan.com
Meat products. Organic meats, exotic meats, smoked and preserved meats, sausages. Phone, mail, or Internet order.

Dean & DeLuca (Mail-Order Department)
560 Broadway
New York, New York 10012
Tel: 212.431.1691 / 800.221.7714
Kitchen equipment and Italian specialty foods.

DiPalo's of Little Italy
200 Grand Street
New York, New York 10013
Tel: 212.226.1033
"Old World" grocers in New York City's Little Italy since 1925, they carry every Italian cheese and food specialty exported. They will ship any product ordered by phone.

Fante's
1006 South Ninth Street
Philadelphia, Pennsylvania 19147-4798
Tel: 215.922.5557 / 800-44FANTES
Web site: www.fantes.com
One of America's oldest and best-stocked kitchenware companies.

Mozzarella Company
2944 Elm Street
Dallas, Texas 75226
Tel: 214.741.4072 / 800.798.2954
Web site: www.mozzco.com
Owner Paula Lambert learned the cheese maker's craft in Umbria. She produces award-winning cheeses made by hand using local ingredients. Products include fresh and smoked mozzarella, fresh and smoked *scamorza*, fresh and smoked *caciocavallo*, and ricotta.

Sur la Table (Catalog Division)
1765 Sixth Avenue South
Seattle, Washington 98134-1608
Tel: 800.243.0852
Web site: www.surlatable.com
Fine kitchen equipment. Catalog available.

Acknowledgments

I could not have produced this volume, which, for its small size, has not been gathered without the efforts of family, friends, colleagues, and strangers alike.

First, thanks to my editor, Bill LeBlond, to my assistant editors, Amy Treadwell and Holly Burrows, and to my agent, Judith Weber, for their many courtesies. For help with recipe testing, thanks go to my mother, Giustina Ghisu della Croce; my aunt, Annette Messina; and my cousin, Diane Messina Miecnikowski. Special thanks to my colleague Ernest Symanski for extraordinary generosity in testing and trying many recipes for this volume, and to my dearest friends Flavia Destefanis and Clarisse Schiller for their constant help with research. I am grateful to Eleonora Paolucci and Corrado Leporatti of La Chiesuola in Bagnaia for their exceptional generosity and hospitality; to Villa Gambara in Bagnaia; to Mary Jane Cryan of Viterbo for her help with research; to Bruce Johnston, Rome correspondent for *The Daily Telegraph,* for the entertaining overviews, and to Fred Ferretti for restaurant recommendations in Rome; to Bill Marsano for wine notes; to Viola Buitoni for the introduction to one of my favorite new dishes and for help with sources; to Giovanni Nonne for his generosity and hospitality in Rome; to Lucini Olive Oil, Bertolli Olive Oil, and La Molisana Pasta for supplies; to Giuliana Quattrocchi of Dal Borgo in Farfa for recipes; to Antonia Scalera of Rome and Acquafondata, and Vittoria Forte of Ristorante Vittoria in Acquafondata for hospitality and help with research; and to Anna Amendolara Nurse, Nick Malgieri, Paul Shaw, and Francesco and Jeanette Sacchini for research; to Sal Ventimiglia of Magna Travel, Maspeth, New York, for research and travel advice; to Eugenia Tice and Ed Shepard of Shireforge Farms, Warwick, New York, for the supplies of organic farm-grown vegetables. Thanks also to Paolo Destefanis for his fine photographer's eye, and for help with research. Last, thanks to my daughters, Gabriella and Celina, for making my trips more fun than usual.

Index

Table of Equivalents

The exact equivalents in the following tables have been rounded for convenience.

Liquid/Dry Measures

U.S.	METRIC
1/4 teaspoon	1.25 milliliters
1/2 teaspoon	2.5 milliliters
1 teaspoon	5 milliliters
1 tablespoon (3 teaspoons)	15 milliliters
1 fluid ounce (2 tablespoons)	30 milliliters
1/4 cup	60 milliliters
1/3 cup	80 milliliters
1/2 cup	120 milliliters
1 cup	240 milliliters
1 pint (2 cups)	480 milliliters
1 quart (4 cups, 32 ounces)	960 milliliters
1 gallon (4 quarts)	3.84 liters
1 ounce (by weight)	28 grams
1 pound	454 grams
2.2 pounds	1 kilogram

Length

U.S.	METRIC
1/8 inch	3 millimeters
1/4 inch	6 millimeters
1/2 inch	12 millimeters
1 inch	2.5 centimeters

Oven Temperature

FAHRENHEIT	CELSIUS	GAS
250	120	1/2
275	140	1
300	150	2
325	160	3
350	180	4
375	190	5
400	200	6
425	220	7
450	230	8
475	240	9
500	260	10